WOMEN

in

CROSS-CULTURAL
TRANSITIONS

**Edited by
Jill M. Bystydzienski
and
Estelle P. Resnik**

Phi Delta Kappa Educational Foundation
Bloomington, Indiana

Cover design by
Victoria Voelker

Library of Congress Catalog Number 93-86990
ISBN 0-87367-478-2 (pbk.)
Copyright © 1995 by Jill M. Bystydzienski and Estelle P. Resnik
Bloomington, Indiana

ACKNOWLEDGEMENTS

This volume would not have been possible without the generous support of the Academic Affairs Office at Franklin College. The Office first funded the Women and Cross-Cultural Transitions Conference in March 1992 and then provided additional funds so that transcripts from the conference could be made during the summer of 1992.

We would like to thank all the faculty, staff, and students at Franklin College who helped in organizing the conference, most notably Dagrun Bennett, Marianna Fallon, Yuriko Ling, Carole McKinney, and Emily Stauffer, who served on the Organizing Committee; Karen Howes and Suzy Nesbitt of Marriott Food Services; Cheryl Mullin from Facility Services; Lavonne Strachman from the Office of Public Affairs; and Jennifer Bostwick and Christie Alexander, who worked registration.

We are grateful for the cooperation and willing involvement of the women whose often painful experiences form the substance of this collection. We also would like to express our gratitude to others whose help was invaluable. Sheron Miller, former secretary to the Dean of Faculty at Franklin College, contributed countless hours, good humor, patience, and technical skill to the preparation of the manuscript. We want to thank Kevin Biesiadecki for his diligent work on the conference transcripts. And we are indebted to many friends, family, and colleagues for their interest in and support of this project.

TABLE OF CONTENTS

Part III

INTRODUCTION

This volume is the result of a collaboration among the editors and the 14 women whose cross-cultural experiences it records. The collaboration began with a one-day conference, titled "Women and Cross-Cultural Transitions," at Franklin College in Franklin, Indiana, in March 1992. It should be noted that the term *cross-cultural transitions* refers to moving across cultures, usually from one country to another or across subcultures within one society. Such transitions extend over a period of time, so that persons involved in this process can immerse themselves in the new cultural environment. Cross-cultural transition also refers to circumstances where people routinely move from one cultural setting to another, for example, when children are brought up with one culture at home and are exposed to another in the community and school.

The morning of the conference focused on women who had made at least one major cross-cultural change or had grown up in a bicultural environment. During the afternoon women students, all in their late teens or early twenties, discussed their own cross-cultural transitions: moving from another country to the United States or changing from a metropolitan, multicultural locale to a small-town, homogeneous environment.

The keynote address, given by Birgit Brock-Utne from Norway, described her experiences of living in several different cultures and pulled together some common themes and issues facing women who have undergone cultural changes and adaptations. Birgit Brock-Utne's revised address is included as a final essay in this book.

Before the conference took place, one of the editors, who was also an organizer of the event, met with the presenters. In these informal meetings, the participants had a chance to learn about each other and to clarify events and issues they would highlight in their individual presentations. After the conference, their presentations were transcribed and edited; and the participants were given the opportunity to revise their statements. In addition, the women students who took part in the afternoon session were interviewed by the editors; and information from the interviews was incorporated into their narratives. These highly personal accounts form the body of this volume.

Why trouble to preserve in print the cross-cultural experiences of a handful of women? We believe that there are several compelling reasons to do so.

Like many other nations of the world, the United States comprises numerous cultures. With the exceptions of native peoples and Africans brought to North America as slaves, whose heritages have been suppressed and nearly destroyed, diverse cultural traditions have continued and even flourished within its borders. These cultures have been brought from all regions and nations of the world, have been transformed to some degree on U.S. soil, and have given America a rich, multicultural social fabric. While documentation of immigrant experiences in the United States certainly is not lacking, much of what is commonly and academically known about the generations of people who came to this country from other lands tends to be simplistic and monolithic. In both popularly held beliefs and scholarly works, U.S. immigrants are portrayed as having homogeneous experiences, as uniform groups or members of undiversified families, frequently not even differentiated by social class, and typically without reference to age or gender (Zinn and Eitzen 1990; Spates and Macionis 1987; Degler 1980).

Only recently have some scholars begun to focus on the subjective experiences of people who have made cultural transitions from various countries to North America and to uncover the great diversity of cultural encounters (see, for example, George 1992; Hondagneu-Soleto 1992; Foner 1987). This volume contributes to that emerging body of knowledge by documenting what individual women perceived, how they felt when they were in the process of moving from one culture to another, and what the consequences of the transition were for them.

The women's experiences recorded in this book also have general implications for the study of cross-cultural transitions. Millions of people have immigrated to or lived for a time in the United States; but people all over the world have made other cross-cultural transitions, either voluntarily or by force. As circumstances impel people to move geographically and culturally, adjustments have to be made; there are gains and losses. As human beings achieve a closer global interdependence, more and more people will make cultural transitions. Thus the personal narratives presented in this volume will be of interest to people in similar situations all over the world.

Those who themselves have made cross-cultural transitions will find these collected narratives engaging. But this volume will prove useful and, hopefully, insightful for native residents who encounter people of different nationalities and from different ethnic and racial groups in their neighborhoods, schools, and workplaces. Those who would like to understand better the difficulties that persons from other cultures experience upon entering a new cultural milieu will find these narratives instructive. The narratives also will interest those persons who want to promote cultural diversity in their communities and to help cultural newcomers feel welcome and appreciated.

A focus on gender is important because relatively little is known about how *women* make cross-cultural transitions. Recently such books as Mary Kay Norseng's *Dagny* (1991), Deborah Keenan and Roseann Lloyd's *Looking for Home* (1990), Eva Hoffman's *Lost in Translation* (1989), Joy Kogawa's *Obasan* (1986), and Maxine Hong Kingston's *The Woman Warrior* (1976), among others, have tried to capture and express what is at stake for women when they move from one culture to another. These books have attracted some attention, but they are rather isolated women's voices. No systematic effort has been made to analyze and interpret their meaning.

This volume presents common themes and issues raised by accounts of cross-cultural transition. Without sacrificing the diversity of women's voices, we attempt to extract from these accounts the shared aspects of their subjective experiences, which allows us to make generalizations that might be tested by future research.

There is a great deal of diversity among women's experiences with cross-cultural transitions; but we contend that women's experiences, collectively, differ from men's. In the majority of contemporary societies, women are socialized differently from men, generally have lower status, and are primarily responsible for children and households (Duley and Edwards 1986). These facts shape women's existence and give women a sense of commonality.

For instance, a combination of low status and specific role expectations – that is, that women be caring and empathetic – makes it more likely that women will see and accept another's point of view and will be less territorial and nationalistic than men. Moreover, women are less likely to feel denigrated than men if, upon entering the new culture, they find themselves in low-status positions, such as working in menial jobs. Thus it may be surmised that women should be able to take on a new culture more easily than men. Indeed, some recent research on Southeast Asian and Mexican immigrants to the United States, as well as on refugees in various areas of the world, has shown that women tend to adapt better and at faster rates to their

3

new cultural environments than do men (Fong 1992; Hondagneu-Soleto 1992; Sheridan and Salaff 1984; Stein 1986).

In Part I of this volume, the accounts by Marga Kapka and Irene Olivier address specifically the issue of sex differences in adaptation to a new culture. Kapka describes vividly the different ways each of her parents approached their transitions from Hungary to life in the United States, and the difficulty experienced by her father, who could not live down the "D.P." (displaced person) label. Kapka's mother, however, despite an extensive education, managed to find enjoyment in a low-status job as a department store clerk and was able to juggle successfully both paid employment and the demands of a large family.

Olivier describes the predicament of the Korean husband/father immigrant who loses power and privilege, and hence personal worth, upon settling in the United States, where advanced age and head-of-household position carry less prestige than in the "old country." His wife, on the other hand, gains power within the family, as well as greater autonomy, as a result of the economic contribution she makes to the household.

Although women seem to adapt more easily than men to new cultures, it is inaccurate to assume that cross-cultural transitions are relatively painless for women to make. Emotionally, cultural changes may be more difficult for women, because they are socialized to "feel" their way in relation to others and the world, while men learn to suppress their emotions (Matlin 1987; Thorne and Luria 1986). Several of the narratives in this book attest to the great emotional sacrifice required by the transitions both groups of women had made.

In Part I, for instance, Dagrun Bennett describes the pain she felt in realizing her loss of belonging, while Marga Kapka and Jean Umemura convey the frustration and conflict they experienced as children living simultaneously in two cultures, being unable to feel full allegiance to either. The evacuation experience was so emotionally taxing for Umemura that for years she was unable to talk about it to anyone, including her children.

In Part II, several of the women point out that in order to adapt to their new environment, they had to suppress what they were feeling. Charmaine Barnard says that in order to function in the new environment, she would "just bury my emotions and not feel anything anymore. A person my age should feel attracted to other people, should have fun, . . . But I was able to cut all that off and not feel a thing. An emotional blank . . . ." Yuko Kanda echoes her: "The way I dealt with my situation during those first few months was to cut off as much of my emotions as I could."

4

For women, the expression of feelings is not only allowed but encouraged. Yet cross-cultural transitions can be so emotionally overwhelming that feelings have to be suppressed in order to function on a daily basis. We are suggesting that it may be more painful for women to do this than for men, since women may have less experience keeping emotions under control.

The experience of moving across cultures may be more difficult for women than men in still another respect. Women frequently have fewer opportunities than do men to become fully involved in the new culture. They often are expected to uphold the values and customs of their cultures of origin, and they may be isolated as homemakers or regarded as mere appendages to husbands if they make the change with their families. Irene Olivier's poignant account of her cultural transition from the Korean-American community in Los Angeles to a small town in the American Midwest tells how, as a housewife, she felt isolated until the birth of her baby. That event transformed her from simply "wife" to the more culturally legitimate status of "mother" and created a vehicle for conversations with neighbors and other community members.

Women frequently rely on other women for support in difficult situations (see, for example, Lenz and Myerhoff 1985), and those making cross-cultural transitions are no exception (Ahern, Bryan, and Baca 1985; Hondagneu-Soleto 1992; Van Reken 1988). The narratives of several contributors, particularly Alwiya Omar and Dagrun Bennett, tell about the importance of women's networks and support groups in the process of cross-cultural change.

These accounts suggest that the study of gender differences in cross-cultural transitions is complex and multidimensional. In some respects, women might make the changes more easily than men; in others, less easily. Women may adapt more easily in terms of daily life situations, such as accepting low-status jobs or balancing family obligations and paid employment; but the emotional price associated with cross-cultural change may be greater for women than for men. For women who move across cultures with adult men, especially husbands, there may be an added problem if they are sheltered from the new environment. On the other hand, women appear likely to find support among other women in the new cultural milieus.

Mercedes Morris Garcia, whose account of moving from war-torn Panama to the United States is included in Part I, coined the phrase, "cultural homelessness." It encapsulates rather accurately the experiences of most of the 14 women whose narratives appear in this volume. Cultural homelessness is a state of being between cultures, of never quite fitting into the adopted cultural environment, but also, having made the change, not being able to slip back easily into one's "home" culture. Thus being culturally homeless implies not having roots anywhere and not accepting wholly the values and customs of any society; in effect, feeling marginal.

Cultural homelessness is illustrated in a number of different ways through these accounts. Dagrun Bennett writes of her "feeling of not really belonging anywhere," of being "lost between these [two] worlds," and of "that easy sense of belonging . . . being lost to me forever." Jean Umemura's confusion about her cultural identity — of being neither truly American nor Japanese — was exacerbated by the evacuation with her family from their home to a Japanese relocation camp during World War II. When Rima Najjar returned to the West Bank after living for several years in the United States, she felt "uneasy" and "invaded" by the pointed stares of the men in the street.

Alwiya Omar recalls visits to Tanzania in which she made "involuntary pragmatic blunders" when she engaged in social interactions. Rika Franke worries about whether she will "fit" when she returns to her native Sri Lanka. Mercedes Morris Garcia and Nicolina Cobo realize that, as professional women, they can no longer feel comfortable in the Latin countries from which they come. On the other hand, they do not quite "belong" in the United States either. Cobo says poignantly, "I don't know where I belong. It's hard because part of me is in Ecuador and part of me is in America, . . . and when I am in one or the other, I am always missing people and things from the other country. . . . I am scared that if I go back to Ecuador to live, I am not going to get used to it. But if I stay in the United States, I will never really have a home either."

For many cross-cultural sojourners, cultural homelessness is the major emotional cost of transition. No matter how successfully they may appear to adapt to their new culture, they never feel fully integrated into any society. Moreover, they can no longer be at home in their culture of origin. Hence, there is frequently a sense of irretrievable loss and rootlessness.

Another emotional cost of cross-cultural transitions is the suppression of feelings that, if allowed to continue, may have serious consequences. Ruth Van Reken, who grew up as a missionary child living in Nigeria and the United States, recounts in her memoir, *Letters Never Sent* (1988), how she learned to build "a wall of good adjust-

6

ment" around her true feelings. She describes the difficulties this attitude created in her relationships with other people. In order to cope with the separation from her parents, relatives, and friends whom she left behind, Van Reken hid her anguish, anxiety, and grief first behind "acting as if all was well," and later in brooding silence and withdrawal.

It took Van Reken many years of painful struggle to come to terms with her suffering and to understand and express her feelings. Many of the contributors to this volume also recall that loss and grief accompanied their transitions to a new culture. A number of them also recount that only through suppression of such feelings were they able to function in the everyday world. Over time, like Van Reken, the older women seem to have reached an understanding of their experiences and to have come to terms with conflict and loss. The younger women have yet to come to that understanding.

Many cross-cultural travelers experience the problem of negotiating a new identity in the host culture. One manifestation of this process is a name change. In the United States and other Western countries, immigrants often take new names, in part to fit in and in part because their own names may be too difficult to pronounce by the Westerners they meet. The Korean Kwanghye Lee became Irene Olivier, initially by changing her first name while she was a student in France and then her last name when she married a Frenchman. Xing Chun Zheng adopted "Alex" as her American name when she discovered that almost everyone she met in the United States found it impossible to say or remember her Chinese name. While such a change may appear to be superficial, those going through the process experience a transformation of identity, including some loss of their former sense of self.

Another consequence of making cross-cultural transitions is intercultural misunderstanding, which may create embarrassment, humiliation, and resentment. Carroll (1988) indicates that such a misunderstanding takes place when "I interpret in my own way an act or a discourse that pertains to a different way of doing things and requires a different filter" (p. 10). The culture one inherits at birth provides one with a culture-bound logic and basic assumptions that one uses to give order and meaning to the world of that culture. Upon entering another culture, one is confronted with a different set of assumptions and logic. However, differences between the two cultures may not be readily apparent. Frequently the cross-cultural traveler interprets the actions and words of people in the newly encountered society based on her or his own native cultural assumptions.

7

A striking example of an intercultural misunderstanding, mentioned by several of our contributors, deals with notions of friendship. Rika Franke, for instance, indicates that in her home culture in Sri Lanka becoming friendly with someone takes time; when people first meet they are polite and courteous. Only as they get to know one another better do they become increasingly friendly. Upon coming to the United States, she discovered that Americans, particularly Midwesterners, are very friendly on first meeting but then make no special effort to sustain a friendship. From her native cultural perspective, Rika expected continued special treatment from people who greeted her in an amicable, effusive manner. When her expectations were not fulfilled, she felt disappointed and hurt. On the other hand, American students who met Rika found her detached politeness to be standoffish. Thus, acting on the assumptions of their own cultures, both Rika and her acquaintances misinterpreted the other's behavior.

As Carroll points out, it takes time and insight to clear up intercultural misunderstandings. Indeed, achieving a degree of detachment from one's own and the host culture and conducting a "cultural analysis" that enables one to become cognizant of the cultural assumptions that intercultural participants bring into social encounters can "transform cultural misunderstandings from an occasional source of deep wounds into a fascinating and inexhaustible exploration of the other" (1988, p. 11). The narratives presented here indicate that cross-cultural travelers with greater experience and maturity provide more sophisticated cultural analysis. While the younger women's accounts are largely descriptive, those of the more traveled and older women seek to explore cultural patterns and understandings. For instance, Rima Najjar describes her struggle to come to terms with the different cultural prescriptions regulating family relations among Palestinians and among Americans.

The narratives in this volume also indicate that moving across cultures offers distinct benefits. All the women point out that their lives have been enriched as a result of exposure to other ways of life and to new and different people and experiences. When they learned to function in the new environment, the women found greater personal strength, autonomy, resilience, and growth.

All six younger women say that they have benefited personally from their transitions. For Yuko Kanda, becoming less shy and able to speak out on issues about which she cares deeply has been a positive development. For Shirley Ann Williams, Jr., the challenge to do well academically in a hostile environment has given her sufficient strength and confidence to persevere. Xing Chun Zheng points out that her travels, first in China and now to the United States, have made her more open-minded, as well as appreciative of her own country.

Charmaine Barnard suggests that even though the transition from New York to a small-town campus in the Midwest was an ordeal, she benefited from the education she obtained, as well as from her increasing involvement in campus activities. And Nicolina Cobo recalls that it took a great deal of courage for her to make the cultural change; but once she did, she gained the confidence to do almost anything.

Feeling alien and marginal in society, while sometimes producing anxiety, has its advantages: It makes one more sharply aware of the shortcomings of that society and helps to develop critical thought. As Dagrun Bennett points out, "When you leave that safe and comfortable place (your own culture), you have to re-evaluate a lot of things." In the end, the person who leaves the safety of "home" not only develops a critical perspective in the new place in which she settles but also brings that critical point of view back to the "home" culture. Stepping outside of one's own society thus opens up the mind to new ways of thinking and looking at the world and is likely to lead to a re-evaluation of one's culture of origin.

For most of the women who share their cross-cultural experiences in this volume, the idealized version of life in America was quickly shattered when they began to learn about and to evaluate their new surroundings. For instance, Rima Najjar comments critically on the materialism that pervades even personal relationships in the United States. Xing Chun Zheng voices her disillusionment with extreme forms of individualism and the superficial friendliness she encountered in the United States. However, both of these women also recognize the shortcomings of their own societies: Najjar, the traditional, restricted roles of women among Palestinians, and Xing Chun Zheng, the excessively hierarchical and collectivistic existence in mainland China.

Cross-cultural transitions entail both advantages and costs. The positive consequences of these transitions are that they tend to lead those involved to develop a global perspective and a critical mind, to acquire the facility to move back and forth between cultures, and to experience enjoyment and appreciation of people from other backgrounds, customs, and traditions. The negative consequences involve pain and grief over inevitable misunderstandings, separations, and losses. It seems that as long as the benefits outweigh the disadvan-

9

tages, or at the very least are in balance, individuals who make cross-cultural transitions are able to live their lives fully and productively, eventually coming to terms with the negatives.

However, a resolution is never reached for some cross-cultural travelers. They may not have the opportunity or insight to work through the dilemma of cultural homelessness or to clear up cultural misunderstandings. They may always agonize internally over what they have gained and lost. Some of these gains and losses are explored by the younger women represented here. However, the experiences of those who are overcome by loss cannot be known, for these students drop out of our colleges and universities. We will never know what obstacles they found insurmountable.

Persons who eventually reach a satisfactory resolution may struggle for years with pain and anxiety before they develop peace of mind about their cross-cultural transition. Support groups and counseling services with therapists specifically sensitized to the problems posed by moving across cultures can help those who are struggling.

Ultimately, educating the public in our increasingly global communities to the dilemmas of cross-cultural traveling and encouraging people to learn from and appreciate those of other cultures would make cross-cultural transitions easier. As educators, we are sensitive to the need to encourage the development of international and intercultural programs. Similarly, we advocate attention to the cultural content in school, college, and university curricula, so that students at all levels are exposed to a variety of cultures and are able to develop an appreciation of cultural differences.

We cannot and should not expect cross-cultural travelers to assimilate – in other words, to lose their previous cultural identity and to fully embrace the new culture. What we may expect and work toward is integration – a mutual accommodation between the newly arrived and the host. Just as a mosaic creates a complete picture out of discrete tiles without disturbing the integrity of each of the individual pieces, so people of different cultural backgrounds also should be able to form an integral community without having to give up their cultural distinctiveness. True cultural integration requires a tolerance for and affirmation of differences, which contributor Jean Umemura calls "a blending of cultures."

It is our hope that this volume will contribute to the newly developing knowledge in the field of cross-cultural studies and help to create more understanding of, and compassion for, the many women – and men – who are cross-cultural sojourners. We are grateful

10

to the women who shared their experiences with us. Their courage and perseverance will be an inspiration to others who have made cross-cultural journeys, as well as to those who have received cross-cultural travelers in their communities.

References

Ahern, Susan; Bryan, Dexter; and Baca, Reynaldo. "Migration and La Mujer Fuerte." *Migration Today* 13, no. 1 (1985): 14-20.

Carroll, Raymonde. *Cultural Misunderstandings: The French-American Experience*. Chicago: University of Chicago Press, 1988.

Degler, Carl. *At Odds: Women and the Family in America from the Revolution to the Present*. New York: Oxford University Press, 1980.

Duley, Margot I., and Edwards, Mary I., eds. *The Cross-Cultural Study of Women*. New York: Feminist Press, 1986.

Foner, Nancy, ed. *New Immigrants in New York*. New York: Columbia University Press, 1987.

Fong, Yuk-Shui Lina. "The Strengths and Problems of Southeast Asian Refugee Families." In *Families East and West*, edited by Phylis Lan Lin et al. Indianapolis: University of Indianapolis Press, 1992.

George, Usha. "Poverty: The South Asian Woman's Experience in Canada." *Canadian Woman Studies* 12 (Summer 1992): 38-40.

Hoffman, Eva. *Lost in Translation: A Life in a New Language*. New York: Penguin, 1989.

Hondagneu-Soleto, Pierrette. "Overcoming Patriarchal Constraints: The Reconstruction of Gender Relations Among Mexican Immigrant Women and Men." *Gender and Society* 6 (September 1992): 393-415.

Keenan, Deborah, and Lloyd, Roseann, eds. *Looking for Home: Women Writing About Exile*. Minneapolis: Milkweed, 1990.

Kingston, Maxine Hong. *The Woman Warrior*. New York: Knopf, 1976.

Kogawa, Joy. *Obasan*. New York: Penguin, 1986.

Lenz, Elinor, and Myerhoff, Barbara. *The Feminization of America: How Women's Values Are Changing Our Public and Private Lives*. New York: St. Martin's, 1985.

Matlin, Margaret W. *The Psychology of Women*. New York: Holt, Rinehart & Winston, 1987.

Norseng, Mary Kay. *Dagny*. Seattle: University of Washington Press, 1991.

Sheridan, Mary, and Salaff, Jane W. *Lives: Chinese Working Women*. Toronto: University of Toronto Press, 1984.

Spates, James L., and Macionis, John J. *The Sociology of Cities*. Belmont, Calif.: Wadsworth, 1987.

Stein, Bernice N. "The Experience of Being a Refugee: Insights from the Research Literature." In *Refugee Mental Health in Resettlement Countries*, edited by C.L. Williams and J. Westermeyer. Washington, D.C.: Hemisphere, 1986.

Thorne, Barrie, and Luria, Zella. "Sexuality and Gender in Children's Daily Worlds." *Social Problems* 33 (February 1986): 176-90.

Van Reken, Ruth E. *Letters Never Sent.* Indianapolis: Van Reken, 1988.

Zinn, Maxine Baca, and Eitzen, D. Stanley. *Diversity in Families*, 2nd ed. New York: Harper & Row, 1990.

PART I

Reflections of Mature Women

The accounts in this section are by seven women, ranging in age from 29 to 66 years. Five of these women were born outside the United States, have resided in the United States for at least two years, and have traveled to and lived in other countries as well. The remaining two were born in the United States and grew up in bicultural environments; within the family, they were exposed to one cultural heritage, while outside the home they functioned in "American" culture. The societies represented by this group of women are Palestinian, Norwegian, Japanese, Hungarian, Tanzanian, Panamanian, and Korean.

The seven narratives present considerable variation in how women experience cross-cultural transitions, but several common themes emerge from these accounts. One is that women face great difficulties when they move from one culture to another. Their status at the time of transition − whether they are single or married, childless or with children − determines the different types of problems they may face. For instance, single women coming from more traditional cultures to the United States are confronted with very different norms governing male-female relationships. Married women with children encounter alien activities and customs, which they struggle to understand but may not want their offspring to accept. Those who were born in the United States and had American friends had to contend with the "differentness" of their parents, whose culture produced a distinctive homelife that was different from the homelife of their peers. Those women whose children were born in the United States, or who came with infant children, endeavor to understand the implications of raising "American" children.

For the five women who came to the United States from other countries, the transition had significant emotional costs. They experienced separation from family and friends, familiar surroundings, and a known way of life. More important, they discovered that, on returning to their home cultures, they no longer fit in easily. They lost a sense of belonging somewhere − they became "culturally homeless."

For the women who grew up in bicultural environments, there was a sense of confusion about which of the two cultures was the primary one. To which culture should they feel allegiance? Only in later years were they able to achieve a sense of peace within themselves and accept both cultural heritages as equally important.

These narratives also show that there is much to be gained from cross-cultural transitions. While all seven women experienced pain, loss, and anxiety, they also developed a great appreciation for other cultures and human diversity. They gained insights into cultural differences, especially about family relationships and friendships.

15

PARENTAL VARIATIONS IN A HUNGARIAN IMMIGRANT EXPERIENCE

MARGA KAPKA was born 22 days after her Hungarian parents arrived in New York in November 1947. Her mother tells of celebrating her first Thanksgiving and eating her first pumpkin pie in the hospital at Marga's birth, thinking surely she was eating something made from soap. The following four Thanksgivings, the family ate in the traditional Hungarian fashion: roast goose with lots of paprika, cucumber salad with lots of paprika, and for dessert, apple or cottage cheese strudel. When Marga was six, she recalls eating cranberries and pumpkin pie. Today she spends less time on turkeys and most of her time teaching writing and literature to high school students in Port Townsend, Washington, where she lives with her husband and son. She owes her fluency in Hungarian to her mother, with whom she exchanges stories and memories. One day she hopes to publish the stories she has collected.

The context in which I will describe the topic of cross-cultural transitions begins with my parents' emigration from Hungary in 1945. My father was 37 when he came to America with my mother and their six children. He knew no English. My mother was eight-months pregnant. They had no friends in the United States, no money, no work.

My father was one of those Hungarians with a fierce love for his country, but whose life was swept out of control under Nazi domination of Hungary during World War II, and more completely under Soviet rule after 1945. His choices were limited to either staying in Hungary and living under the Soviets — who expressed their power through Stalinism at that time — or emigrating to America. Because he loved Hungary and hated oppression, neither choice appealed to his basic instincts. With five children, my parents left Hungary illegally and secretly for Belgium, where they resided for two years and where another child was born. In Belgium, the hope of returning to Hungary never left my parents. But the post-war scare of Communist expansion throughout Europe eventually convinced my parents to go to the United States.

Three weeks after they arrived, I was born. I'm seventh in a family of 10. I have always felt that my birth was a pivotal event in the history of my family's life. My parents called me "Lucky Seven" because my birth as an American citizen allowed them to make the United States, rather than Venezuela, their home, in spite of the fact that the quota for Hungarian refugees had already been filled. Their visa had been originally for Venezuela.

Because my father never really felt "at home" in the United States, I have sometimes thought that the timing of my arrival was less than fortuitous. But we do not choose things like the time of our birth or the time our country goes to war; and, like both my mother and my father, I feel I've coped with and been confused by an ambiguous situation.

Getting to America was a hardship in itself. With my mother eight-months pregnant, my parents, their six children, and my grandmother bartered and bargained for passage on a steamer leaving from Antwerp to New York. In my mother's mind, as in the minds of many refugees, visions of America as the land of gold beckoned enticingly. As the ship drew into the harbor, my parents gazed reverently at the Statue of Liberty, an imposing sight on that cold, clear morning of November 1st. My father knew it was an important moment. He held my mother and whispered in words mixed with relief, sadness, and promise: "We left behind old Europe, and we'll start a new life."

"Give me your tired, your poor, your huddled masses yearning to breathe free . . ." is the soothing message of the nurturing, colossal lady to all the uprooted who enter America by way of New York — all those immigrants who said goodbye to their homelands. On the one hand, America did give my parents refuge. In reality, however, my father encountered daily discrimination that betrayed the suspicious feelings many Americans harbored against foreigners during the late 1940s and early 1950s.

When they landed, my parents, along with other refugees, were met by Traveler's Aid representatives, who handed out sandwiches on white bread and candy bars to the children waiting to pass through customs. My mother felt relief at being out of the ship's berth, which the three adults and six children had shared with a Polish couple and their two children. My father was jubilant and energetic. "How thoughtful these Americans are to bring us food," he remarked to my mother. And, although he was unable to speak the language to express his gratitude verbally, he smiled. They passed through customs and, again assisted by Traveler's Aid, they found a hotel where they could stay until their transit visa expired.

They knew nobody. My father had only one address, that of a Catholic priest who lived on the East Side, in the Hungarian section of the city. Unable to speak a word of English, but with a confidence that surprised even him, my father set out to find this priest. The subway station around the corner provided a helpful guide; my father found a German-speaking passenger who gave him directions. He walked whenever possible, avoiding the risk of having to ask directions for riding buses.

Trusting his intuition, he made his way to the Hungarian neighborhood where he found the church and the priest. Talking to the priest delighted my father. They conversed in Hungarian; and the priest assured him that because of my birth, the family would be permitted to remain in America. Not only that, but my father would also be able to obtain a refund from the steamer ticket they would have used to go on to Caracas. The priest gave my father the name of a hospital where many of the physicians were from Eastern and Central Europe. He told him not to worry and that he would help him find a job.

As he left the church, my father was brimming with joy. But in his excitement, he lost track of the subway station. Puzzled, he looked around, trying to focus on something familiar; but all the tenement apartments looked alike. Approaching a small cluster of people surrounding a bus stop, he tried to look for facial features that spelled "immigrant" but felt confused searching these foreign faces. Utilizing every language he knew, but unable to speak the only one that mattered now – English – my father asked a man for directions.

"Aw, shaddup, ya' damn DP!" the man spat at him.

The designation DP, for displaced person, never must have seemed more apt.

Later, I remember being nine years old, sick with flu and lying on the living room couch, listening to my mother's quiet kitchen noises – not the usual scrubbing of dishes, but rather the rustle of newspaper pages being turned. I loved it that my mother retreated to the large, warm kitchen to read after everyone else was asleep. Tonight was no different. She was waiting for my father to come home from

19

work. He would be making the long drive home after working all day on the trains in Cleveland. I thought of words my father had recently spoken over Sunday dinner.

"Your father is the best diesel mechanic in the train yard. He can smell out any trouble with the trains. This is why he is gone so much of the time. Even on his days off, the yard superintendent will call and say, 'John, I know it is your day off; but we cannot get this engine to run. *You* are the genius around here. Can you come?' And, of course, your father goes and finds the trouble immediately. He knows more than the others."*

Finally the sound of my father's old car filled the driveway, and then the familiar smell of diesel fuel penetrated the kitchen. I detected sadness in his voice as he greeted my mother. I heard the clink of a bottle and knew they were sharing a glass of wine. My father began talking.

"They don't like it that I know everything about the engines, so they laugh at my English. So I want to learn better. When I take a book to read, to study, to learn the language, they laugh at me because I spend my lunch hour reading. Imagine, today I had to climb atop an engine; and as I was bending over to inspect the injectors, they struck a match to the oil rag in my back pocket."

Tears filled my eyes, and then I felt rage. Then I felt sorry for my father. I got up and went into the kitchen, wanting to be included in the moment. But when my father saw me, his weariness vanished, and his eyes intensified with surprise and anger. He wanted to know what I was doing out of bed; and despite my mother's explanation that I was sick, he banished me to my room, with a stern admonition that nine-year-olds should be sleeping by this time of the night. I crawled into bed, my heart hurting more than my stomach, unable to let go of the image of my father's rear end in flames.

Increasingly, my father realized that finding a new life meant abandoning his former life – his identity as a Hungarian. But the more he recognized that success meant embracing a new culture, the stronger he resisted acculturation. When my father was home, he lectured us endlessly about the lack of spiritual and cultural substance in American life. He delivered resonating tirades about the politics of greed, whose chief exponents were the Soviet Union and the United States. Constantly, he reminded us of how his own country – his home – had been "negotiated," parceled out and destroyed by the

---

*Editors' note: In the Hungarian language, third person singular is the formal manner for talking about oneself.

20

politicians. First at Trianon in 1918, after World War I, there was the dissolution of Austria-Hungary as a major power. Then again at Yalta, following World War II, there were Stalin, Churchill, and Roosevelt, who stripped Hungary of yet more land.

One day, I was curled up in a chair reading Ian Fleming's latest James Bond thriller. I didn't notice my father's anger until he was standing in front of me. "Oh God," I thought, dreading the next moment. "What is it going to be this time?"

My father neared, his eyes ablaze but his voice low and controlled. He showed me the Franklin Delano Roosevelt stamp which he had meant to apply to an envelope. Then he thundered, "Do you think I would lick this stamp? Do you think I would lick the man who ruined my country? Bah! No! I spit on that man!"

He spat on the stamp of FDR. And he continued with his condemnation of the dead American president who in 1945 negotiated the Yalta Agreement.

"There he sat with Stalin and Churchill and, just like a pie, cut up Hungary! This piece is for you − that piece is for me!"

My father's voice became louder as he described the helplessness of his country, the injustices it suffered, and the resulting obscurity of its genius. "DO YOU UNDERSTAND WHAT I AM SAYING?" the Hungarian words shouted at me.

"Yeah, dad, sure, dad," I mumbled in English.

He glared at me. "When you are in your father's house, you speak your mother tongue; you speak in Hungarian to your father. DO YOU UNDERSTAND?"

"Yes, father, I understand," I enunciated in Hungarian.

I longed to say to him, "If you hate it so much here, why the hell did you ever come?" But I didn't dare.

In contrast to my father's often-voiced intolerance and opinionated approach to carving out a new life in America, my mother did not express her viewpoint on cultural identity. She spoke Hungarian with us, but she was also very interested in conversing in English. Unlike my father, who pretended not to understand if we said something to him in English, my mother actively engaged us in discussions so she could practice her English.

She also began reading books and newspapers voraciously to improve her comprehension. She was very busy raising 10 children, although my older sisters contributed enormously to helping my mother. The duties of motherhood insulated her from the dangers − perceived and real − of surviving in a strange world. For 10 years we lived in rural northeastern Ohio, a haven for children; but for my Belgian, boarding school-educated mother, a woman who spoke four languages, it was a test of faith, courage, and sheer willingness to assimilate. She had nothing in common with the neighbor women, but she never held herself aloof.

When I was eight years old, my mother had to go to work to make ends meet. She woke up early with my father, and he drove her to a meeting point where she shared a ride with four other women who worked at the same department store in Cleveland. My father then continued the 50-mile drive to the railroad yard in another section of Cleveland. They both finished at the same time and came home together around 6:30 p.m. My sister and I stood by the window facing the road, waiting for the headlights of my father's old Plymouth.

These few months that my mother worked I recall as a vague gap in my childhood. My mother represented fulfillment and stability. With her gone, the house was empty; the home had no hearth. She worked from the end of summer until Christmas, but her absence lasted an eternity. When Christmas finally came, it brought not only the usual yuletide merriment that year, but also the comfort and joy of my mother quitting her job and staying home with the family once again. She quit because my father simply did not want her to continue working. Despite the tremendous financial pressures on him, which her meager paycheck did help alleviate, he wanted her home. I wanted her home, too.

Only several years later, when our family moved back to Cleveland and I met some of my mother's former co-workers, did I realize what work meant for her. She had made many friends; she was praised for her work. She used her foreignness as an asset. Customers returned, requesting the small woman with the "adorable" accent who was cheerful and who knew so much about the merchandise.

My mother's willingness and ability to adapt to a new culture makes sense in light of her upbringing. She was the only child of a mother who at 18 moved to Budapest from Vienna and a father who was a respected Jewish neurologist. She was sent to boarding school in Belgium at the age of 10, where she learned three other languages in addition to studying English. My mother did not want to leave her home in Budapest in 1945; but once the decision was made, she looked to the future more than the past. She approached obstacles with a cooperative attitude, rather than the confrontational and competitive behavior of my father.

How did these different approaches to assimilation affect me? I grew up with conflicting messages about cultural identity and allegiance. When I became old enough to perceive the "differentness" of our family, I was embarrassed. I rejected my mother tongue and my Hungarian heritage because I associated my father's unwillingness to be tolerant with being Hungarian.

In 1956, following the October Revolution, my teacher expected I would choose Hungary as my special project country; but I didn't. How could I possibly convey to my fifth-grade peers what it meant to me? What sense could I make of my father's joy as he danced around the kitchen with my mother, laughing that the bloody Communists would be kicked out and would rot in hell. And, after the tanks moved into Budapest 10 days later and it was clear that no aid would be sent to the Hungarian freedom fighters, how would I ever have been able to explain my father's dark anger and the storms that erupted from him when he listened to the news. I was confused because I didn't understand the politics, but I was certain in not wanting to be associated with that country in any way. I wanted it to just disappear.

As a university student, I socialized with international students, including a few Hungarians. I enjoyed my association with them, although I felt I liked them first because they were fine individuals. I never forgot incident after humiliating incident in which my father had placed all his trust in an insurance man, for example, just because the man was Hungarian, only to be swindled or taken advantage of.

I also took linguistics courses and became interested in the Hungarian language and in the culture.

My first trip to Hungary four years ago with my mother (after my father's death) reinforced my perception that acculturation doesn't necessarily mean severing your roots. My father's approach left him in a no-win situation. He was convinced that if he learned to become American, he would forever lose his identity as a Hungarian. There was no middle ground between the two choices.

My mother, on the other hand, adapted to, rather than rejected, American culture. Yet even today she maintains her connections with relatives and friends in Europe. After having lived in America for over 40 years, she still reads, writes, and converses as well in Hungarian (and French and German) as in her adopted language, English. For her, the commitment to acculturate presented an enriching challenge rather than the threatening and bitter isolation it presented to my father.

Personality enters into how people adapt, but transitions can change people. In conversations with my mother, she has described my prewar father as an opinionated young man, but one whose sense of justice included compassion and whose tolerance and patience were second nature. In post-war America he was an immigrant, a foreigner, a DP. He arrived in New York with six children, his pregnant wife, no sponsor, and no job. He was an educated man, a man versed as well in the poetry of Sandor Petofi as in the mechanics of diesel engines. He had an opinion on everything; he breathed politics. From the deck of the Liberty ship which carried my parents away from their homeland in 1947, my father had uttered words of promise to leave behind old Europe and start a new life.

But my father never left old Europe. Unlike my mother, who built a bridge between her two worlds, my father's heart broke in America. Still, he endured because his convictions were rooted in a deep faith in God, in my mother, and in the decency of human life. From both of them I have received an inheritance: my mother's strength, my father's passion.

PROUD TO BE A
JAPANESE-AMERICAN

JEAN UMEMURA was born in Seattle, Washington. Her parents came to the United States from Japan and originally planned to stay for just a few years, until her father made enough money. Instead, they remained in the United States and had three children. Jean attended elementary and junior high school in Seattle. Just as she started high school, World War II broke out and all persons of Japanese ancestry living on the West Coast were forced to move into government relocation centers. Jean and her family lived in Camp Minidoka in Idaho for two and a half years. Eventually, her parents secured jobs in Ann Arbor, Michigan, and the family was able to leave the camp. Jean obtained B.S. and M.S. degrees in education and taught elementary school for almost 30 years. She has three children, four grandchildren, and is retired. She and her husband, also of Japanese descent, reside in Indianapolis, Indiana, and are active in the Japanese American Citizens' League.

My parents came to the United States from Japan, which makes me an American of Japanese ancestry. However, for a long time when I was growing up, I felt confused about whether I was truly an American or a Japanese. I grew up in an all-Caucasian neighborhood, predominantly German, Scandinavian, and English. In most ways I felt very American. My first name is Jean, my twin brother's name is John, and my older sister's name is Mary. How much more American can you be with names like that?

I attended a high school that was all white except for one Asian face other than my brother's and mine. All my friends were Caucasian; and I felt so American that whenever someone would tease me and call me "slant eyes," a Jap, or "flat nose," I would run home feeling very offended. I would look in the mirror and, as I examined my face, I would say to myself, "I don't look Japanese at all. I know I don't." As I look back on this now, I think that I was denying my Japanese identity because in my heart I felt so American. I didn't believe my eyes or my nose looked any different. The children who had called me those things had to be wrong!

Then there were times when the doors of our home were closed and just my family was inside — dad, mother, sister, brother, and I — and we would speak Japanese rather than English. My parents found it easier to speak in their native tongue, and they preferred that we use Japanese at home. Occasionally we did use English, but within the family we usually spoke Japanese.

Every day after dinner, the three of us children had to sit down at the table and learn to read and write Japanese. Before she married, my mother was a teacher in Japan; and she taught us herself. I remember thinking how arduous it was to learn the language. I preferred to use English and wished that my parents could speak it more fluently. I was ashamed of the broken English they spoke to my friends, neighbors, and customers at my father's dry cleaning establishment. As I grew older, I became aware increasingly of how different my parents were from those of my schoolmates. They spoke differently and their mannerisms were different. This embarrassed me at times.

When I was 10 years old, my siblings and I sailed with our mother to Japan to spend the summer there. The purpose was to meet our relatives for the first time and to expose the three of us to our parents' homeland. We enjoyed our trip immensely, being able to experience firsthand everything Japanese. However, I did not feel as if I belonged in Japan. I felt different because I spoke American English, I dressed like an American, and my mannerisms were American. I noticed that children in Japan seemed quieter than American children. They even giggled quietly. They were reserved and obedient. I was not boisterous or loud, but I did have an outgoing personality.

All the Japanese children even had their hair cut the same way. The girls had straight hair and bangs, and the boys had theirs shaved very close to their heads. My hair was styled and curly. I had a distinct appearance and personality. I welcomed returning to the United States and home.

My life seemed to be going along smoothly, following everyday established routines. I was taking piano and dancing lessons, my brother was in Scouting, and my older sister took violin lessons. My father wanted to show his appreciation for all the work the teachers in our elementary school did to educate the three of us. He had us present two Japanese cherry trees to be planted on the school grounds before my brother and I graduated from the sixth grade. From then on, we were known as "the Japanese cherry blossom twins."

I loved Judy Garland and Mickey Rooney movies because they were so American. I could hardly wait to grow up and attend high school just like the one Judy and Mickey went to in *Strike Up the Band* and in the "Hardy Family" movies. These films were made in the late 1930s, before the United States became involved in the Second World War, and were very popular.

Pearl Harbor day, December 7, 1941, changed our lives. The next day, President Roosevelt declared war on Japan. As I sat listening to him on the radio in my high school auditorium, I could not help feeling embarrassed and sad. Was everyone looking at me? I wondered. Did my classmates think my relatives had anything to do with Pearl Harbor? Was I supposed to feel bad about being Japanese? Was half of me, the Japanese side, ashamed? Was the other half of me, the American side, proud? As I reflect on those years of the war, I know I had to be confused and ashamed at times; proud and resentful at other times.

Shortly after Pearl Harbor, the United States government ordered all people of Japanese ancestry to be evacuated from their homes if they lived along the West Coast. They were placed in 10 different camps in several states: Idaho, Wyoming, Utah, Nevada, Eastern California, Arkansas, and Arizona. The camps were located in desert areas and came equipped with guards and barbed wire.

Life in Camp Minidoka in Idaho, where my family was incarcerated for two and a half years, was not easy for me. The fact that our lives were so disrupted and completely changed from what we were used to had a great deal to do with my difficulties. For one thing, it was an adjustment to live among only Japanese people after having been around mostly Caucasians. The lack of privacy was a very important problem. I could not just retreat to my room or to any room in our new abode if I wanted to be alone. Our new accommodations consisted of one small room in a barracks where many other families lived. In order that we might have some privacy, my father put up wires between the beds and my mother hung sheets on the wires like curtains.

To pass the time constructively at the camp, we got involved in various activities. At the beginning, it was important that we all pitch in and help in any way we could so that the new community of 10,000 people could function. I worked in the mess hall, where over a hundred people in our block had to eat. My job was to help prepare baby food. Later, I got a job in the administration building doing some typing and filing. I practiced on the piano in the recreation hall so that I could continue my music study. Before too many months passed, teachers from outside the camp were hired; and a school was started for first to twelfth grades.

The camp school I attended was called Hunt High School. It was not a large brick building like the high school back home in Seattle. It was located in barracks filled with tables instead of desks and was woefully short of supplies. The school system was rather makeshift; and equipment of any type, whether it be for science laboratory classes or cooking or sewing classes, was scarce. We had few textbooks and often had to share them. College preparatory courses were very limited, making it difficult for those who might have wanted to go on with their educations.

I remember trying hard to stay optimistic and to look forward to a better future. It was very difficult, since I had no idea when my family and I would get out of this camp. There were times when I was happy trying to lead a "normal" teenage life; but also there were times when I was very depressed, feeling that being Japanese had ruined my teenage years.

After two and a half years, my parents were able to secure jobs with a dry cleaning firm in Ann Arbor, Michigan. It was necessary that my parents have jobs and a place to live before the government would allow a family to leave the camp. My parents had to make arrangements to live away from the West Coast, as we were not allowed to return to the coast while the war was still going on. In Ann Arbor we found a small apartment and a new beginning for all of us.

My siblings and I resumed our education. Eventually, both my sister and brother attended and graduated from the University of Michigan, and I graduated from a teachers' college in Michigan not far from Ann Arbor. I married a Japanese-American who, like myself, grew up on the West Coast and was evacuated with his family to a camp during World War II. We have three children; two were born in New Jersey and one in Indiana after we came to live in Indianapolis 36 years ago. Throughout most of these years, I taught in the local school system while my husband was employed in market research by a major pharmaceutical company. We raised our children in an all-white neighborhood, and they attended predominantly white schools. Two of our children are now married, one of whom, a daughter, has four children, and one, a son, has one child.

My husband and I did not teach our children very much about our Japanese heritage, nor did we tell them about our experiences in the camps. However, one day our son came home from school and asked whether we knew anything about the Japanese-Americans who were evacuated from the West Coast during World War II. He had read about it in a paragraph in his history textbook. For the very first time, my husband and I then talked with our children about the evacuation experience. The children were surprised to learn that we had been forced to disrupt our lives to stay in the camps.

We were somewhat relieved by our disclosure, as we had not spoken about this time to anyone. I am not certain why we kept silent about the past all these years. Perhaps it was because we led busy lives and we lived in an environment that included very few other Japanese-Americans. I know that we went through an emotional upheaval during those years in the camps; we felt a lot of shame and we were deeply humiliated. After getting out, we just wanted to leave it all behind; and I suppose we suppressed the memories as well as we could.

We felt ashamed of being Japanese because we were made to believe that we did something wrong to be placed in the camps, that we were disloyal. As an older, more mature person, I now know that we did not do anything wrong; the United States government was wrong in evacuating us. It has taken me many years to come to this realization.

During the last 15 or so years, largely because of my teaching experience, I have become interested in my heritage and have studied more about it. My husband and I took a trip to Japan in 1976 and visited the relatives I met when I was 10 years old. We hope to go to Japan again soon, not only to renew the relationship with our relatives but also to learn and understand more about our heritage.

When prejudice against Japanese people was strong in the United States, my husband and I were reluctant to speak about the evacuation experience. However, as the country began to accept more the different cultural backgrounds of its people, it became easier to discuss my life at Camp Minidoka.

While we did not expose our own children to Japanese culture, now we are trying to teach our grandchildren some of the things we failed to teach our son and daughters. It is heartening for us to see that our grandchildren are growing up feeling at ease with the knowledge and better understanding of their Japanese roots. We also have joined a chapter of the Japanese American Citizens League, an organization that has helped us to develop pride in our cultural heritage.

When I was younger, half of me would feel Japanese, the other half American. I would go through periods of confusion, asking myself, "Am I American, or am I Japanese?" Today I feel more comfortable about the blend of the two cultures. I no longer see the two as being in conflict, but rather view them as rich strands of my life that I can draw on and weave together into beautiful, intricate patterns. I feel at peace with myself when I say that I am an American of Japanese ancestry.

A FRANCOPHONE KOREAN
IN AMERICA

IRENE KWANGHYE LEE OLIVIER was born in Seoul, South Korea, and graduated from Korea University with a B.A. in French language and literature. She attended graduate school in Paris, France, and obtained an M.A. in linguistics. After finishing her Ph.D. coursework, she decided to join her French husband, who was working in Southeast Asia. They relocated several times in East Asia and moved to the United States in 1991. They spent a year in the Midwest and recently settled in Fort Collins, Colorado. She now is raising her son and plans to resume her work toward a Ph.D. as soon as possible.

Readers might wonder why a Korean would have a Western first name. My Korean name obviously is not Irene but Kwanghye, which means "grace of light" or "bright grace." The reason I have a Western name is because I chose to be called Irene rather than having to hear Kwanghye being badly mispronounced. Kwanghye has a very strong "h" sound; and the French, who typically avoid pronouncing the letter "h," could not say my name correctly.

Moreover, I noticed in school that since it was so difficult for non-Koreans to remember my name, they simply did not call on me and sometimes even avoided talking to me. After a few weeks in France, I decided to find another name for myself that Parisians could say easily; and I picked Irene. Changing my name was indeed my first and major cross-cultural transition.

The first foreign culture I had contact with was not American, but French. Fourteen years ago, when I graduated from the university in Korea, I decided to continue my studies in French literature in Paris. At that time Korea was quite different from what it is today and was considered an "underdeveloped" country. The government did not want a lot of people to go abroad to spend foreign currency, which was so precious for the economic development of the country. Also, in Korea as in many Asian countries, it was more difficult for a female to leave and study abroad than for a male. Girls were meant to receive a decent education and to get married soon afterward.

31

In my case, it was my mother who helped me a great deal to go on with my studies, because she once wanted to have a college education herself but could not. As a girl she had to sacrifice herself for the education of her brothers. She wanted me to have the education she had missed. In order to get an exit visa, I had to take an exam given by the government. I passed the exam and soon left for France with my mother's blessing and joy.

My life as a foreign student started in Paris in June 1979. I was miserable at the beginning. Even though I had studied French for four years, my French was poor; and I didn't know anyone in Paris. Not only did I miss my family in Korea, but the weather in that city was usually very depressing. The sky was gray and it often rained. Paris looked very empty in July and August because, as I found out later, it was summer vacation time, when most Parisians go south to enjoy the sun.

When these Parisians came back from their month-long holiday all fresh and tanned, they were no help in my solitude. Parisians have a very special attitude, not only toward foreigners but also among themselves. They look on others they do not know with total indifference. One cannot meet an eye even in a packed subway station. It was as if they looked at the wall through you.

Once school started, I could meet other students and could follow the lectures. In the end, the transition to Paris wasn't that bad. First, because I made a lot of effort to adjust myself to French society, since I had chosen to go to France instead of staying in Korea, and second, because I lived in a very privileged environment, the academic world. Usually people in academe tend to be more open and interested in many things. And finally, French people are, in general, very generous to those who want to learn about their culture and civilization. Overall, I enjoyed my stay in France very much; and I could even say that I adapted quite well.

While I later lived in several Asian countries, my second important cross-cultural transition took place when I came to the United States. I arrived in Los Angeles at the beginning of 1991 in totally different circumstances. I accompanied my French husband, who had quit a stable and well-paid job to come to America to continue his studies. This time, I didn't have as much culture shock. I think I became much wiser and much more experienced after having lived in a number of different countries.

My husband and I first met in Korea when I was a senior at the university, but our lives criss-crossed for many years afterward. I went to France after graduation, and he had to stay in Korea to continue his studies. We got married in Singapore, where he was later sent by his multinational Swiss company; and right afterward, I went back to Paris to continue studies toward my M.A. He was then sent to Taiwan while I was in Paris, starting my Ph.D. in French linguistics, which I have not yet finished. He was in Seoul when I was again in Paris for an intensive training in interpretation and translation for the Seoul Olympic games.

In fact, when my husband went to Los Angeles in 1987 to resume his Ph.D. in history, I was in Seoul working for the 1988 Olympics. My job, as a simultaneous French-Korean interpreter, was to attend all the conferences and meetings before and during the Olympic games and to translate the documents and letters in French and Korean. After the Olympics, I joined my husband in Beijing, China, where he was doing his doctoral dissertation research. Finally, we decided it was time for us to start a normal, married-couple's life; and two years later we came to the United States together.

Los Angeles has a very big Korean community. Accidentally, we found an apartment in the middle of Koreatown, which has a population of about 70,000 Koreans. It is like a little city all by itself. I even felt sometimes that I was back in Korea. There is not only everything one could need to cook Korean food, but also many Koreans who cannot speak a word of English. I could manage fairly well in the English language. While English was never a working language for me, it was taught in Korea beginning in junior high school and always was one of my favorite subjects.

Living in Koreatown offered me several advantages, such as providing easy access to Korean supermarkets for food and finding a job easily even though it was not legally permitted at that time. (I did not have the required "green card.") As for my husband, a Frenchman – and a Chinese and Korean historian who has lived in various Asian countries for close to 10 years and is fluent in Korean – he did not have any difficulty communicating when he lived in Korea. However, he had to face the same problem in Koreatown in Los Angeles that he faced in Korea. That is, he had to deal with a certain animosity from the Koreans whenever he talked to them in Korean. They would look at him full of suspicion or with barely disguised contempt and answer him in English, if they could. This was because most Koreans thought that foreigners who spoke Korean must be either priests or GIs who married Korean prostitutes. Moreover, American GIs do not have a very good reputation among Koreans.

This attitude has been amplified in Los Angeles by the fact that Koreans there live in a very closed community.

Overall, my husband's transition to American culture has been rather smooth, I think, for some of the same reasons mine was when I first went to Paris. His English was much better than my French had been when I arrived in France, and he was already a very cosmopolitan person.

In Los Angeles, I worked as a journalist and staff writer for a Korean-language monthly magazine published locally. This magazine aims at giving information about American society, the education system, and other institutions to help the newly arrived Korean immigrants. While I am not sure of the specific number, a lot of Koreans immigrate to America every year. Problems caused by cultural integration are one of the main topics of this magazine. Working on the magazine enabled me to see very closely the difficulties faced by Korean families in America.

When Korean families move to the United States, it is usually the older adult males who have the most difficulty adjusting to the new culture. There are several reasons for this. First, the Korean society where they were born and raised has totally different values. In Korean society, as in other Confucian societies, one's status is determined by age. The more advanced the age, the higher the social status. If you are of a certain age, you have a position that everybody knows, and you belong to a well-defined category. But when Koreans come to America, this social standard no longer works and the older men are no longer in a special position.

A major reason Korean males have difficulty in the United States results from the work they take on in order to earn a living. Very often Korean immigrants have to work in small businesses, which is the lowest kind of work by Confucian standards. Confucius is a Chinese philosopher who lived in the fifth century B.C. His ideas of a strict social hierarchy that extols scholarship and education and looks down on business activity had a tremendous influence on Korean society.

According to Confucius, there are three categories of jobs that ordinary people can have. (Scholars, nobles, or aristocrats, who are not considered "ordinary," have their own standards.) The most respectable job is farming. The second category is work in industrial production. Business comes last and is the lowest category, because in business, one must handle money all the time. In traditional Confucian thinking, money is something very low that people with noble spirit should despise. Of course, in modern society it doesn't work that way. But this tradition is very much alive in the minds of Koreans.

Thus, Korean immigrants in business are usually not very happy about what they are doing. For example, when my husband decided to quit a very well-paid job in business to join the academic world to become a professor, which is the most respectable job one can have according to traditional Confucian standards (in the past only aristocrats could become teachers), my parents were very pleased and congratulated him, even though they knew the pay would be totally different and our standard of living would fall dramatically. While he is not even Korean, my parents, who are strongly influenced by traditional Confucian thinking, applied their own values even to a Frenchman.

Another reason Korean men experience difficulty in the United States is the change of power in the family. Korean society is very patriarchal. According to traditional Confucian thinking, fathers in the family are equal to kings. That means fathers have total power and control over family matters. However, when they come to America, this structure of power starts to change. Very often fathers have the kind of language problems that their children overcome very quickly. Wives work outside the home, which gives them a certain financial independence and, consequently, more voice in family matters. Korean fathers most often accept this change only with great difficulty and resentment.

You might ask, then, why do Koreans immigrate to America? I am not certain why, but it is not typically for economic reasons. Very often Koreans come with enough money to start a small business. It is most likely for family reasons. Koreans usually have very strong family ties. If one member of the family is in the United States and becomes successful, he will invite other, less fortunate, family members to come to America to try their luck. After all, America has the reputation of being a country with plenty of opportunities.

Koreans also may immigrate for social reasons. Korean society is highly competitive. For instance, a friend of mine has a boy who is six years old. The boy's day starts very early in the morning with lessons about how to answer the phone in English, because you have to learn English to be "better" than others. Later he goes to a swimming pool to exercise his body. He comes home directly after swimming, and a music teacher waits for him to give him a piano lesson. In the afternoon he learns drawing, calculating without a calculator (because it is supposed to increase brain power), and so on. He is provided all these activities so that he can become better than the other boys. And the competition goes on and on. Most Koreans get used to this kind of competitive life and to handling the pressure, but some don't like this lifestyle and want to escape from it. That may be why they immigrate.

I mentioned that I didn't have severe culture shock when I came to America, but that does not mean life in the United States as a foreigner has been easy, even now. After a year in Los Angeles, my husband and I moved to a Midwestern town, where he got a teaching job in a small college. I felt very isolated; and even though people generally seemed friendly, I could not get close to anyone.

I find it extremely difficult to make friends with Americans, especially close friends with whom I can exchange more than, "You look great," or "Let's get together someday." Perhaps I expect too much from friends, or do I expect something different from friendship? In Korea, friendship means a total commitment, somehow without saying a word about people's feelings. A close friend would never tell you, "you look great," but you just know by his or her way of talking that he or she thinks you do. Koreans would exchange comments such as, "You look great," or "Let's get together someday," only if they were with people they did not know very well and they felt obliged to say something.

In fact, revelation of one's feelings is quite rare in Korea. I never saw my father holding my mother's hand and telling her how much he loved her. Rather, he would say, "You look so tired today. You should sleep the whole afternoon." This kind of comment does not offend anybody, and my mother knows that he says this because he loves her and cares about her. Nor did I ever see my mother telling her grandchildren how lovely they look. Instead she would say, "You, little piggy, are just growing fatter and fatter every day," but with a beaming smile which said everything. I have some difficulty in accepting a different way of manifesting one's feelings and friendship.

But something happened recently that has given me new hope. I had a baby boy born in 1991, and he is playing the role of intermediary between me and American society. When I go out with him, I feel the ice around me start to melt. Without him, I could stay in a shopping mall a whole day by myself and nobody would talk to me. But when I am with him, a lot of people approach me and want to talk. Isn't it marvelous?

And most importantly, I feel now that I belong to an important category in America. I belong to the noblest category that exists in the world, that of *mother*. Even though I've been living away from Korea for 14 years, I am still very Korean. I get a secure feeling from belonging to a meaningful category in another society. And once I feel secure, I think I can contribute to society in other ways as well as by being a mother.

A PALESTINIAN'S STRUGGLE WITH CULTURAL CONFLICTS

RIMA NAJJAR is a Palestinian who grew up on the West Bank of Jordan. She studied at the American University in Beirut, Lebanon, for five years and has traveled to Syria and Kuwait. Before coming to the United States, where she obtained a Ph.D. in English literature, she taught English at a Palestinian refugee camp in Amman, Jordan. She is married to an American, has two children, and currently resides and works in Bloomington, Indiana.

Although I have American citizenship and, more importantly, I have American children (a boy who is now 13 and a 10-year-old girl), I still think of myself as a Palestinian. Perhaps because of the difficult conditions my people have had to endure, I feel my Palestinian identity is indelible. I know only too well what it means to be a Palestinian. I am still sorting out what it means to be an American.

I came to the United States to get a higher education when I was 24 years old. I stayed three years, obtained my degree, and went back to Jordan to fulfill a contract with the government, which had subsidized my education. The man who is now my husband, an American, followed me there. We got married; and after spending three years in Jordan, we came back to the United States, primarily because my husband was finding it difficult to adjust to the Palestinian culture – a culture where the extended family unit was a force with which he needed to come to terms. My husband did not wish to participate in an endeavor that was fraught with complex emotional demands, but it was impossible for us to live there isolated from such complexities. After much heart-wrenching deliberation, we packed up and left.

My initial experiences in the United States as a student and as a single woman were buffered, of course, by the campus and by a structured, goal-oriented existence. I was already well-educated; and through literature and the various media, I felt I had a good knowledge of American culture. This knowledge, like that of most newcomers to America, was vastly idealized; and the adjustments I had to make were of the down-grading sort, especially in relation to the political system. The equity and ringing promise of the United States Constitution were not often visible on the daily TV news. And the people running everything were men, just as they were back home.

One difficulty at that time sprang from the fact that I had been studying Western literature and tradition, from which I felt alienated. I had a similar experience when, in my teens, I attended a boarding school run by German nuns in Jerusalem. The after-effects of the British colonial mandate in the area were still evident in the 1960s. We studied a syllabus designed to prepare us to pass a British exam. We read Jane Austen, Charles Dickens, and Shakespeare at the expense of our own rich literary tradition, which was neglected. That course of study was guaranteed to instill a deep sense of alienation and inferiority in us. No matter how hard one tried, it was impossible to genuinely admire, for example, the image of "a host of golden daffodils" except as a mythical construct, because one wasn't even sure what a daffodil looked like. But the high value put on that literature and tradition came across loud and clear.

I later went on to obtain a B.S. degree in biology and a master's in English at the American University in Beirut. I then returned to Amman, Jordan, and taught English to Palestinian refugees. Within a year, I was offered, and took, the opportunity to travel to the United States to earn a Ph.D. in English literature with the guarantee that a university position would be available to me on my return.

At the American university, where I received my doctorate in English literature, I felt like a fraud, even though I was able to crank out the required papers and to read the required lists of books with apparent competence and facility. I expended a lot of energy pretending I wasn't a fraud, pretending I had an intuitive insight into a body of literature largely represented by white British and American men but very few women of color.

On another level, the issues that I struggled with had to do with my social interactions. Behavior norms regulating relationships between men and women were clear and inflexible in my culture. In the United States, I was a 24-year-old woman who had just started to struggle with issues of "dating" and sexual intimacy, issues that most Americans work out in their teenage years. All of a sudden, I had freedom. But it was strongly tempered with ingrained perceptions of what is proper behavior. As a result, I was still severely restricted in what I would or would not do.

Nevertheless, my cross-cultural experience in this regard has been an unequivocal gain for me. I know that the women's movement in this country has yet a long way to go; but compared to the restrictions on women my society has, this culture is liberating. I still remember how I felt when I first went back home after finishing my studies here. I had been very homesick and took the earliest opportunity to get out and walk around, savoring familiar sights and smells. As I walked, I felt more and more uneasy as I realized that every man I passed on the street was taking the time, leisurely and pointedly, to examine me from head to foot. I had gotten used to assuming the "license" of walking in public without having to worry about the routine, overt scrutiny of male eyes, or about the ingrained assumption that a woman has little business strolling in public unaccompanied by a male escort. Involuntarily, I started wondering whether I was not properly covered or whether my walk itself was perhaps too jaunty and unrestrained. It was a terrible sensation that hastened my steps back home.

When I returned to the United States as a married woman and a mother, I initially assumed that, given my previous experiences in this country, I would encounter little or no culture shock. That turned out to be an optimistic assumption. Once again, I found myself struggling with issues primarily having to do with relationships: my relationship with the members of the family I married into, my relationship with neighbors, and my relationship to the country. Most of all, I struggled to understand what my children's American identity meant.

In families here as elsewhere, social interactions are directed and nurtured by women. That was the case in my family, and it quickly became apparent that my husband was not going to be much help. He would have been perfectly content if we lived as a nuclear family with as little social interaction with the outside world as possible. I therefore had to learn things on my own — sometimes from television, and you can imagine what that meant!

In my culture, behavior norms among family members are well-defined. This, of course, has its stultifying restrictions and drawbacks. But it does have the virtue of somewhat simplifying life. In the United States, I had to learn that as the son and oldest sibling in his family, my husband and, by extension, I had no special responsibilities. In a Palestinian family, the oldest son is groomed at an early age to become the head of the extended family. He is given every privilege, according to the means of the family, with the expectation that, as an adult, he will care for his aging parents and younger siblings, especially any unmarried sisters. There were no such expectations, or expectations of any kind it seemed to me, in my husband's family.

For example, my husband insisted that we did *not* have to invite his family to Thanksgiving dinner every year. "How does it work then?" I asked, and he couldn't really explain. I still have no idea; every year Thanksgiving is full of suspense and surprise.

It appears also that my husband has no obligations toward his nephews other than buying them birthday and Christmas presents. His sister, to this day, carefully offers to repay us financially any time an occasion arises in which we even casually extend ourselves on behalf of her son. My husband's father offers him money for the temporary use of our truck. I struggle to understand that all this does not necessarily mean that their relationships are cold and mercenary. These exchanges are just a different way of doing things.

In my interactions with my neighbors and friends, what I initially missed sorely were some forms of behavior that expressed hospitality and regulated one's interactions as a host and as a guest. At first, I reacted with hurt to casual behavior on my neighbors' part that really was not meant to hurt me. After knocking on their doors for one reason or another, I was sometimes not invited in to transact whatever business took me there.

If I was asked in, I was often not offered any refreshments; and when I was offered something and politely refused, I was taken at my word and not offered whatever it was again. As a child, I was taught never to accept the first offer of anything and to wait until I was asked again, possibly several times, by the person making the offer. This allowed the recipient to gauge the sincerity of an offer, as often the rules of generosity compelled a host to offer all kinds of things to a guest, whether the host could afford to do so or not. Even the innocent practice of *asking* a guest if he or she wished to have something to eat or drink instead of simply offering it seemed appalling to me.

When we lived in Jordan, my husband had the opposite problem. He interpreted people's efforts to express their hospitality to him through the repeated offering of food as a continual infringement on his right to refuse what was offered.

I struggled not to take these things personally. When someone knocked on my door, I missed the formulaic words of welcome my language offered in abundance and found equivalent phrases, such as "Please come in," painfully lacking.

All these things may seem silly, but their underlying message about the ways in which people care for each other, if misunderstood, is serious. I am still trying to resolve such basic issues as what it means in the United States to be a neighbor, a friend, a sister-in-law, or a daughter-in-law. It seems to me that here one is free to invent and reinvent such identities, and there are as many answers as there are families or neighborhoods. That is precisely why it is difficult for a foreigner to work things out.

Some time ago, a neighbor asked my son if he would feed and exercise her dog while the family was away. She offered to pay him five dollars. When my son related this proposition to me, my immediate reaction was to tell him that he should, of course, help out, but that he should not accept money from a neighbor for helping out. My son felt cheated of a great opportunity to make money and accused me of being un-American.

My position was that by accepting money, my son would be transforming "neighborliness" (something I valued) into a business transaction. My son wanted to know the precise radius beyond which the neighborhood, in my mind, dissolved into the world of promise and opportunity. In the United States, children do make money by doing chores for neighbors. Both television and my husband confirmed it. The neighbors would have felt beholden and refrained from asking again if they had not been allowed to pay my son for his "work."

I put my foot down on having to pay my son for doing chores around his own house, though. But is his house really his? Is my and my husband's money also my children's? Not according to the Cosby show, the most "wholesome" family show on television.

The idea of ownership was something that, as the mother of young children in America, I had to sort out. I remember the shock I felt on hearing other mothers reinforce their toddler's natural instinct of wanting to hold on to a certain toy for dear life by emphasizing the idea of ownership. They insisted that since the child owned the toy, he or she should have the freedom to decide whether to share it or not — that is, it was good to share, but acknowledging the child's sense of ownership and, therefore, of power and mastery over the material object he or she owned was more important. Though I admired the sure way these mothers enforced this creed — and it is undeniably a capitalistic, if not a fundamentally American creed — I am still uneasy with it.

In my culture, children are socialized at an early age to share what they have with siblings, cousins, and friends; and they are shamed when they don't do so. The idea that what one has also belongs to others in the family is ingrained so thoroughly that I remember, as a child, asking one of my aunts if taking something from a sister without that sister's knowledge — I had my eye on a glittery object she possessed — could possibly be considered stealing. I was sure it would be technically impossible to judge it as stealing in the same way one cannot be said to steal from oneself.

When my daughter needs to use something that her brother owns, I want there to be a strong presumption, one that is stronger than the right of ownership, that she can use it. That willingness to share also applies to sharing with a friend in need and with a stranger in need. In the end, it also applies to sharing with Haitians in need.

The culture conflicts I have experienced must surely have influenced my American children, must have even confused them. I have mastered the art of baking an apple pie, but the secrets and joy of baseball are still beyond my grasp. One thing I did learn from base-ball, however, is the huge importance of competition in the United States. It is safe to say that, as a rule, women from all cultures are less comfortable than men with competition. But as both I and my son painfully discovered, doing your best in American culture is not enough, not even in Little League baseball. One has to be better than the next guy if one wants to play at all. This tenet applies to people just as it applies to goods.

Next summer, I am taking my children to visit their relatives in Jordan. I have recently wondered what, if anything, is going to set my children apart from their cousins there. With their pumped up shoes, fluorescent shirts, and electronic gadgets, clearly my children will be the more accomplished consumers, the material Americans — the hip, gum-chewing, trendy Americans. This much is clear. But will they also be the loud and brash ones, the enterprising ones, the ones who go after what they want, no matter the cost? Will they be kind and generous and open? Will they be the smart-alecks, the go-getters? I don't know. I am still trying to work out what it all means.

A ZANZIBARI WOMAN'S REALIZATION OF HER MOTHER'S DREAM

ALWIYA S. OMAR was born on the island of Zanzibar in Tanzania. She has studied in Kuwait and has traveled to Saudi Arabia, Madagascar, and the Comoro Islands. She was on study leave from the University of Dar es Salaam from 1987 to 1993. She recently completed a doctorate in linguistics at an American university and returned to her homeland to teach at the University of Dar es Salaam. She is married and has three children; her husband and two oldest children currently live in the United States.

My mother was born and raised on Zanzibar, an island that became part of Tanzania in 1964. When she reached 10 years of age she was no longer allowed to play outside with her friends. Neither was she allowed to go back to school that year. Even though she did not care very much about playing outdoors, she cared about school. She could not understand why she could not go on to third grade when she did very well in school the year before. She felt she was being deprived of something important. She decided then that if she were to have children, whether they were sons or daughters, she would not prevent them from going to school; this became her dream.

My mother was lucky to have received two years of elementary schooling. Her mother had no formal education whatsoever. My mother came from a strict Islamic family where women and girls who had reached puberty were not to be seen by men who were not married to them. In my maternal grandfather's time, boys were not sent to school either; but my grandfather managed to go to school by pretending to visit his aunt every morning. The aunt was sympathetic and encouraged my grandfather to attend school without his parents' permission. After several months his parents discovered this but allowed him to continue anyway.

When he graduated from school and started working, my grandfather, together with some colleagues of his, founded a school. In his mind, my grandfather wanted to encourage boys' education. As it turned out, in order to show a good example, he had to send his daughter to school because he had no sons. My mother attended school for two years, and then my grandfather decided that it was time for her to stop.

My mother was married when she was 18 to a man she met for the first time on her wedding night. The man she married, my father, was an Arab from Yemen. He was never able to acculturate to the way of life of the people of Zanzibar. He left Zanzibar after his seventh child was born.

My mother's dream of sending her children to school was not realized easily. She was not able to send her eldest daughter to school because she could not argue against her father's or her husband's wishes. She had no problems with her second and third children; they were boys. With her fourth and fifth children, her dream of educating her daughters came true. My sister and I attended school. My mother did not get any resistance from my grandfather, who was old at that time, or my father, who was about to leave Zanzibar and did not succeed in getting custody of us.

Even though my sister and I were able to attend school, we were not allowed to play outside with other children once we turned 12. We also had to wear the veil. We used to sneak outside to play anyway and got reprimanded later. At this time I made up my mind that if I were to have daughters of my own, I would not restrict them from playing outdoors.

My mother's resolve to educate her children no matter what it took resulted in abolishing the unwritten rule in our family of not educating girls. My mother saw to it that all her children, sons and daughters, got educated. If it had not been for my mother, I would never have gone to elementary school. If it had not been for her persistence and encouragement, I would not have gone through secondary school. And if it had not been for her and my uncle, I would never have been able to venture to travel internationally to Kuwait, where I attended a four-year college and earned a B.A. degree in two years in English literature and linguistics.

Traveling to Kuwait was the first time I had ever traveled alone. I was 24 and had not gone anywhere by myself while I lived in Zanzibar, until I graduated from high school and started teaching. Then I could walk alone from my home to school and back. The Indian

Ocean was just a short distance from where our house stood, but I grew up not knowing how to swim.

Going to Kuwait meant leaving the family protection, the over-protection, I had had all my life. By no means was I let go abruptly. My uncle came with me as far as Nairobi, Kenya. The next transfer was in Cairo, and my uncle arranged for his friends to come get me at the airport. Then, when I arrived at Kuwait City airport, officials from Kuwait University were there waiting for me and that was just as well. I do not know if I would have been able to find my way to the university. I would have been scared to take a taxi, since I arrived at night. I did not know any Arabic then. I would not have been able to communicate with anyone. I did not think of all these things before I left Zanzibar. I was confident that with my strict up-bringing, everything would be fine. My mother and uncle felt the same, otherwise they never would have agreed to my going anywhere where I would have had problems.

Actually, I was very helpless but determined not to show it.

I had to make major cultural adjustments while I lived in Kuwait, even though Kuwait is an Islamic country like Zanzibar. I had to learn how to live in a dormitory with a roommate. I had to learn to keep warm during the winter season. It did not snow, but it did get cold; and I needed to wear sweaters, a coat, and all the necessary accessories.

The first year was bad. My Arab roommate was always complaining about whatever I was doing. It seems that our customs and mannerisms differed greatly. It was impossible for us to communicate and to discuss these differences; she spoke little English, and we did not know each other's native languages.

The following year, life became better. There were three East African women in the same dorm. When one of them graduated, I moved in with the other two. Without the support of my East African roommates, I would have had a tough time in Kuwait. I learned a great deal from them. I also met my first American friend in Kuwait. From her I learned something about the United States and its people.

After the two years in Kuwait, I traveled to Madagascar and the Comoros. I got married and started raising a family. Then I went back to school at the University of Dar es Salaam in Tanzania to obtain an M.A. degree in linguistics. After graduation, I secured a faculty position at the university.

The idea of coming to the United States materialized one day when I was talking to an American colleague in my department at the University of Dar es Salaam. My colleague was holding a letter and asked me, "Do you want to try this?"

"What?" I asked.

"Apply for a Ph.D. program in linguistics at an American university. Read this," my American colleague replied.

The letter that my colleague showed me was from the coordinator of an African Language Program at a large university in the American Midwest, asking my colleague to look for an individual who was interested in pursuing Ph.D. work in linguistics and who could also teach Kiswahili. I had been teaching in the Department of Linguistics at Dar es Salaam for one year when that letter arrived. At a university where the motto is "publish or perish," one would take any opportunity that arose to enable one to complete doctoral studies. Upon completion of the studies, promotion was certain; a Ph.D. ensured the position of a lecturer, the equivalent of assistant professorship at an American university.

I thanked my friend and wrote the African Language Program coordinator at the U.S. university to say that I was interested. I had already told my husband that I was going to enquire about the possibility of going to the United States. It was my husband who actually urged me to write and ask for details. I did not think anything would come of the enquiry; but to my surprise, I eventually was accepted into the Ph.D. program. I talked to my mother, and she, remembering her dream about the sky being the limit for education, thought it was a good idea. She promised to help my husband in taking care of our children. My mother was a great help when I was working on my master's degree, too. What would I have done without my mother? My uncle and the rest of the family were behind me one hundred percent, also.

With the encouragement of my husband, my mother and others in the extended family, and of my American friends, I once again made a long trip, longer than that first one to Kuwait. It took me two days to get to Chicago, where I spent the night in a hotel room because I had missed my connecting flight. The next day, when I got to my destination, the African Language Program coordinator was at the airport waiting for me. From the airport we went straight to a workshop for African Language instructors.

That was how quickly I moved into the system. From then on there was no slow moment. The pace was faster in the United States than anywhere else I had been. This fast pace was the first thing I had to adjust to. In Tanzania the rhythm of life is much slower and more relaxed. People are expected to take their time when they meet relatives or neighbors. Even if I may be on the way to an appointment, should I run into someone I know, I am obliged to stop and talk with the person until we are both satisfied that we have caught up on our mutual whereabouts. If I am late for my appointment, so be it.

Moreover, once I get to my meeting, I do not discuss its purpose until my colleague and I have shared information about our families, mutual friends and acquaintances, our opinions on the current state of the world, and so on. A considerable amount of time should pass before we get to the reason for which the appointment was made.

At the beginning I thought I would not be able to survive for long doing all the things I was expected to accomplish in my new university situation. It was the first time in my life that I had to teach and study at the same time. But miraculously, I managed very well. I think this fast pace helped me not to dwell on the fact that I had left my family behind. There was no time to feel homesick. It was difficult, but I had the consolation that my children were in good hands and were getting all the love they needed from different sources: their grandmother, their aunts and uncles, and their father. I vowed to telephone them once a month.

An American friend of mine remarked on my ability to leave my children in my mother's care. She felt that this was an option for African women that American women usually do not have. African women are able to take advantage of career opportunities because typically there is the extended family to attend to child care and other female responsibilities. The extended family is a resource for working women in many parts of Africa.

In addition to the fast pace, I had to learn the appropriate use of language. That is to say, I needed to be aware of the cultural values of the American people in relation to the way they use their language. I discovered that it was not necessary to shake hands whenever I greeted someone I knew. I learned that it was socially appropriate to go straight to the main topic of conversation without first exchanging lengthy routine formulas about the well-being of the other, as is the case in a Kiswahili-speaking community. I also learned that one is expected to write "thank you" notes and to say "please" when making a request. In contrast, the emphasis in bringing up children in my community is on greeting properly and not on saying "please" and "thank you."

After I had lived alone in the United States for two years, my husband and my three children came to join me. Through my children

I learned about American customs. I learned about the tooth fairy tradition one morning when I had the following exchange with my seven-year-old son:

"Mom, my teacher told me to put the tooth under my pillow and the tooth fairy will come and give me a dollar. But there's no dollar here," he called out.

"Maybe the tooth fairy will come tonight," I told him.

He was disappointed but put the tooth back under his pillow. That night I crept into my children's room and put a dollar bill under my son's pillow. The next day he was happy and excited and showed the money to everyone.

Back home in Zanzibar, children are told to throw the tooth onto the roof of a neighbor's house. The tooth fairy tradition is one tradition I have come to accept. I do not know what I will do when we go back to Tanzania and my last born starts getting rid of his baby teeth. Will it be the tooth fairy or the neighbor's roof?

There are other traditions that I also have come to accept; the carving of pumpkins is one. My children carve pumpkins every year at their honorary American "grandmother's" place. They wear Halloween costumes and go trick-or-treating. In allowing them to do all this, I am fulfilling my dream about not depriving my children of joy and fun, of doing things that other children enjoy doing.

Even though I have accepted the tooth fairy and the Halloween traditions, I have resisted accepting others. For example, I told my children that Santa Claus will not come to our apartment and that they cannot go to the mall to talk to Santa Claus. Christmas is part of Christianity, a religion in which I was not raised. I come from a strict Islamic family, and therefore there are limits to which I can relax rules. However, my children can help family friends decorate their Christmas trees. Decorating a tree does not mean going against the Islamic tradition, even though I find it impossible to do it in my own house.

My main concern now is the transition all of us, my husband, my children, and I have to make when we go back home. I think especially of my 13-year-old daughter. I am going to try to convince my mother to nullify the veil rule so that my daughter will not have to wear it in Zanzibar. But she will not be able to wear shorts when she goes back, however hot the weather becomes.

My children are already thinking of what they are going to do when they go back to Zanzibar. They intend to open a candy store and a fast-food store like McDonald's. Anticipating the slower pace of life, they think they are going to have plenty of time on their hands!

Since I came to the United States almost five years ago, I have been back to Tanzania twice for short visits. I discovered that I can no longer slip back easily and comfortably into my home culture. While I still enjoy the not-so-fast pace of life, I am afraid that occasionally I've appeared rude and unfriendly when I performed involuntary pragmatic blunders: I did not readily shake peoples' hands; I forgot to greet an older person by using a respectful greeting form; I went straight to the main topic of conversation, forgetting about obligatory opening exchanges. I know that when I return with my family, there definitely will be another period of cultural transition for all of us as we resume our lives in Tanzania.

EXPLORING CULTURAL HOMELESSNESS: AT HOME HERE, THERE, AND NOWHERE

MERCEDES MORRIS GARCIA, from Panama, has been in the United States since 1990. She worked for five years as a journalist in her native country during the Noriega regime, which she actively opposed. She has studied in Panama, Mexico, and the United States and has traveled extensively in Europe, the United States, and Latin America. She is completing her doctorate in mass communication and development at Indiana University. She now lives in Connecticut with her British husband while completing her dissertation on the cultural and communication aspects of adolescent pregnancy prevention in eight Panamanian communities.

Although I am from the Central American Republic of Panama, I often feel culturally homeless. Some of it has to do with the fact that I am not as dark skinned as my compatriots and do not have a noticeable Latin accent. People I encounter often expect me, as a Latina, to look and act differently. As genetic luck would have it, I don't look as Latin as my siblings. And my years of education abroad have all but eliminated my Spanish accent. I have come to learn that there is something to be said for physical, racial, and ethnic identifiers; they play an important part in who we think we are. Mine have led to reverse cultural stereotyping.

Born the eldest daughter of a U.S.-born father of British extraction, who was raised in Panama, and a Panamanian mother from a traditional family extending back to the Spanish colonial period, to some degree I experienced cultural conflict within my childhood home. For example, political tensions between Panama and the United States over issues of sovereignty and the canal were often painfully internalized in our family.

Although I traveled extensively throughout the United States and Europe when on holidays, my first real encounter with an extended

53

cross-cultural transition took place when I was 19 years old. I moved to Zacatecas, Mexico, to attend a school of veterinary medicine. Although it was my language the people spoke, I was unable to translate or to fathom the squalor and social inequity I witnessed there.

My second transition took place on entering Loyola University in New Orleans in the United States. I was quickly assimilated by the group of Latin students; but we then realized that by maintaining our primary cultural allegiance, we were defeating the purpose of an education abroad. My group expanded to include U.S. and other international students. As I progressed through my courses, most of my Latin friends seemed uninterested in and even derided the academic and intellectual issues that I found so fascinating. This conflict was the first break in my changing perception of myself and what I saw as an unwanted, culturally appointed role in which academic or intellectual pursuits were not welcome.

Upon completing my studies I returned home for what I thought would be a month-long hiatus before resuming studies as a graduate student in the United States. The political situation, however, drew me into working as a journalist and writer in opposition to the dictator Manuel Noriega. I then stayed home for four years.

As the only woman journalist at *La Estrella de Panama*, I experienced a transition of another sort: I entered a culture of predominantly male journalists. Once again, I encountered issues of culturally appointed roles. These reinforced my perception of myself as a professional woman who really did not conform to Panamanian cultural expectations. I don't want to suggest that all Latin women are relegated to rigid roles, but this was the way it appeared at the time.

When the Noriega crisis finally exploded in mid-1987, I became a stringer and correspondent for a number of different international news organizations; and like many other journalists and opposition Panamanians, I was also persecuted. Before Panama's 1989 elections and while I was setting up a media center for foreign journalists to transmit news from Panama, I was briefly jailed. Noriega was trying to maintain media silence during the elections, and my actions undermined his.

A year later, in 1988, I began working at the U.S. Southern Command as a press officer and spokesperson until the U.S. military operation ended in mid-January 1990. It was at this post that several events caused new cultural and gender conflicts within me. For example, the Southern Command was a U.S. organization to which I had to maintain loyalty, regardless of my Panamanian identity. Furthermore, it was a male-oriented military organization, not exactly the warmest place in which a professional woman could find herself.

I left Panama after the U.S. invasion, suffering from a mild case of suppressed post-traumatic stress disorder, probably a result of my jail stay; and I headed for Harvard, where I started graduate studies and where I found it difficult to meet other Latins. I had no support group to substitute for my lost home, a home which had now been further transformed by the presence of U.S. troops, which I had a hand in welcoming. Coming from the tropics, Boston seemed very cold, culturally as well as climatically. The unfamiliar winter weather made it extremely difficult to adapt; and I would not go out for days, trying to avoid the discomfort I felt wearing so many layers of clothing.

The academic community was not very welcoming either, and I felt alienated within it. I found myself constantly defending my past job as a press officer for the U.S. military and felt that I had entered a hostile political environment. The transition was so abrupt that I felt unable to stay in Boston and chose to leave, electing to come to Indiana University to pursue a doctoral degree. I.U. offered a scholarship and an associate instructor's position within my preferred field of study, mass communication, whereas at Harvard I had been in political science.

I was in Indiana between August 1990 and 1993, my first time in the Midwestern United States, something to which it took me about 18 months to adjust. I had now lived in three distinct U.S. cultural settings: the South, the East, and the Midwest. The change in economic status was also a blow, from a well-paid professional position to a graduate student meagerly supported by the university.

As with previous changes in my life, among the things that made this transition so difficult were, I think, my own conflicting attitudes and behaviors. It is difficult to hold close both the values and behaviors associated with being a professional academic woman trained in the United States and the values and behaviors of my primary cultural milieu of Panama. Without either, I cannot feel at home. But embracing both creates an internal uneasiness.

The Western feminist traditions, which I have studied and embraced, also conflict with my own cultural traditions. For example, professional women here do not usually wear their fingernails long. In Panama, professional women do; in fact, it is considered unsightly for women to have short fingernails. Patterns of networking are different as well. Here, I believe women network with each other. In Panama, women must network more with men and less with women, as usually occurs in *machista* societies. Other cultural differences come in terms of male-female relationships. In Panama, for example, men usually insist on paying for dinner or the movies, whether on a business lunch or a date. In the United States, "going Dutch" often is the norm.

Human relations also differ tremendously between the U.S. and Panamanian cultures, which makes it difficult to make American friends. To be seen as a successful and well-adapted person in the United States, one is expected to maintain a certain distance, be self-sufficient, assertive, and even aggressive in some cases; never weak or needy. This is not the case in Panama, or, I would suggest, in many other more traditional societies, where the successful person relies on a more openly visible extended network of support from family and friends. Unlike the predominantly nuclear families in the United States, families in Panama are both close-knit and extended, and women play an important role in keeping families close.

In Panama, and in many traditional cultures struggling with both post-modernism and U.S. cultural "invasions," I've found an unbridgeable gap between what is expected of a woman professionally and what is expected of a woman romantically. These are deeply incompatible positions. We have an entire generation of professional women in Panama in their 30s caught in the period of transition from a traditional to a post-modern culture, many of whom have not and probably will not marry as a result of this larger societal transition.

But I have been dwelling on what is culturally different about us while neglecting that which makes us globally very much alike. We all have been in touch with a worldwide, post-industrial, post-modern culture. This culture actually has made our transitions possible and even has encouraged them. The post-Cold War period is characterized by a shifting world order, open borders across many nations, and increasingly service-oriented economies that are replacing industrial and agricultural economies. There is something to be said about the bonding power of this overarching culture that we share.

My thoughts on these global issues have given me a chance to address some important personal ones that I've kept "in storage" for many years. My personal insights center on what I may have in common with other women and on what sets us apart from one another culturally.

A good part of our perception of ourselves grows from our interaction with others. It is in the light of how the "other" sees us and in his or her reaction to us that we form our views of ourselves. When the "other" does not automatically place us in the ethnic and racial category to which we feel bound, and in which we expect to be placed, we are left feeling somehow separated from our own cultural group without feeling that we are part of the "other's" group. As a result, we feel culturally homeless.

Cross-cultural transitions are so difficult precisely because the transitions require us to conduct this kind of self-examination, and we do it while living in another culture, feeling under a microscope in view of the "other."

In today's "global village," there seems to be an abundance of cultural permeability. Cultural boundaries are crossed by millions of people every day. Many of us live beyond the boundaries of our homeland, forever longing to recapture the security and warmth of our lost childhood home and of our own cultural group. Our home seems lost to us after the many small and large cultural transitions we have made. Those transitions change us so deeply that when we do return "home," we feel that we no longer belong. To throw off these uneasy feelings, we may try various mental strategies: We find fault with our own ethnic group, our culture, our homeland, and we embrace instead the virtues of our most recent home and culture. Once we leave home again, all of these feelings begin to recycle. In that sense, then, we may literally think ourselves into cultural homelessness.

What is so deeply disturbing is that we continue to be afflicted by this feeling of homelessness. And that is, I suggest, an inescapable condition once we cross certain cultural boundaries. Cultural homelessness is the very thing we have in common in post-modernity. It brings us together while keeping us apart. But it is not to be confused with hopelessness. Cultural homelessness can also be construed as a form of belonging to many different cultural settings. Thus we can belong to as many cultures as we encounter.

That which can prevent homelessness from becoming hopelessness is acceptance and even celebration of our multiplicity of cultural allegiances. Perhaps it will help bridge the gap between "self" and "other."

LOST AND FOUND

DAGRUN BENNETT grew up in Norway. She traveled extensively in Europe before coming to the United States. She is married to an American and has three children and two grandchildren. Since the late 1960s she has lived in central Indiana, where she is director of computing services at a small college.

When I came to the United States for the first time in 1959, it was not my first experience abroad. As a 15-year-old I spent the summer at a school in Denmark that my mother and grandmother had both attended; at 17 I spent the summer in England; and at 18 I went to Switzerland for five months and then to France for eight months. This is not unusual for Norwegians. Even though it might seem that, at the geographical outskirts of Europe, Norway must be isolated from the rest of the world, the country has a long tradition of seafaring and trading, and young people are expected to want to explore and learn about the rest of the world.

Norway is second only to Ireland in the percentage of her population to have emigrated to the United States. When I married an American, I did not have to deal with the terrible racial and cultural opposition that many of my friends from other countries talk about. My Vietnamese friend Dzung was told by her father that if she married an American, she would still be welcome in his house, but her husband and children would not. My parents, after the first shock that I wanted to marry at 20, welcomed my husband into the family with warmth and graciousness. Later, however, I did have to deal with their anguish when my husband and I decided to move to the United States.

In 1959, a couple of months before our first child, John, was born, my husband went back to the States. When John was 4½ months old, we joined him. I had already been through all the first-time shocks of trying to understand another culture, such as the isolation of not understanding the language. Since I was married to a native, I had someone to explain and interpret the mysteries of everyday customs

59

and colloquialisms. But there were still many that threw me — like the time we invited some neighbors to dinner and she called to ask if they could have a "raincheck." Or the time I held out my hand to say goodbye, and the hostess looked at it as if it were some sort of strange animal. (In Norway we shake hands a lot.) Anyway, there are the little things that bothered me, but that I had to expect and learn to live with when I left home. It helped a great deal that our first next-door neighbors were French and American. Blanche had been in the United States for 13 years; she had her own long list of faux pas, and she helped me to laugh at mine.

There are other things that stand out in my mind now as truly perplexing to me when I first came here. This country was still caught up in the McCarthy-era attitude, with its intolerance and paranoia. I expected that, because the rest of the world knows a great deal about what goes on in America. What impressed me was the absolute certainty that all the answers to the human condition had been found — right here. There were solutions to all problems. If you did the right thing, God would reward you with material wealth; consequently, if you did not have material wealth, you must not be good.

With a background in war-time and post-war Europe, this did not fit my world view at all. I was amazed that people my own age had this unbounded optimism that there was nothing they could not do. They seemed to see things with such clarity; they were strangers to soul-searching and doubt. I had grown up with people whose mettle was truly tested — some of them were heroes in a very quiet, unassuming way — and my friends and I always felt that we could never measure up.

But what I really want to examine is not the process of adapting to a new culture, but the slow realization that comes after many years, of things found and of things irretrievably lost, and of the balance one hopes is there. It is not clear to me anymore if there is a difference in the way women perceive this final reckoning. I used to think that men adapted more easily and more completely; that women were more closely tied to the family they had left behind and never fully accepted the separation. The published letters and diaries of Norwegian emigrants support this, and so do prose and poetry. It was Beret who went crazy in the North Dakota winter in *Giants in the Earth* by Ole Rolvaag, and in Ingeborg Refling Hagen's poem, "In a Chicago Hospital," it is a woman who pleads to get well enough "to go home to die."

Last summer when she was going through my grandmother's papers, my sister found a letter that my grandmother received in 1893 from a male friend who had gone to Wisconsin, and it is clear that it was not so easy for the men, either. Although he had found work and could see that "being careful it is possible to put something aside," there is throughout the letter a sense of abandonment. He was a stranger in a land he did not understand, and the bridges to the familiar had been burned. The letter is a plea for contact and support. I wonder if he found it.

In many ways I am more fortunate than most, because my husband loves my country and my family. He learned to speak my language, and he enjoys spending time in Norway. I come from a very close-knit family, and we have stayed close in spite of the distance. As the oldest in the family, I have a special relationship to my parents; and that has never changed. Maintaining this closeness is more important to me than it is to my sisters. I understand that, and it is all right. My mother also knows it. One of my sisters told me that Mother made her promise to write to me when Mother no longer can.

For a while it was five years between my visits home, and one of my nephews was four years old before I saw him. But lately I have been able to go home once a year. I am very fortunate. I know that and I am grateful for it every day.

It was when my children were teenagers that I first began to think of "loss." There had been confusion a lot of the time, and homesickness at certain times. Sunshine on a bright, snowy day is agony for me. But the sense of loss came with the realization that my children were different from me in a way they would not have been had we stayed in Norway. So much of who we are and where we fit comes from who our heroes are. I know the American heroes (and some of them puzzle me), but nobody here knows mine. A few people may know who Fridtjof Nansen was, but not how his courage and humanitarian compassion inspired my dreams and imagination. Only historians know that Trygve Lie was the first Secretary General of the United Nations. For all Norwegians this means that a small country can make a large contribution, because the ideas nurtured by the need for cooperation can transcend military hardware and the power play of large nations. It gives us a sense of relevance beyond our numbers.

All cultures have shared images that are evoked by trigger words, sayings that mean much more than just the words themselves. Whole national identities are summed up in a song or a flower or a name. Even though I know better, I find myself saying, "In Norway we have a saying. . . ." It always loses in translation, because the shared knowledge that makes it meaningful is not there. Norway is a homogeneous country; things pretty much mean the same thing to everybody, and so it is very comfortable to know that what you say will be understood the way you mean it. At home I could not hurt someone's feelings and not know it, but that has happened to me here. There is a lot of talk right now about the different modes of communication of men and women. Add language and cultural background to that, and it can be a recipe for real loneliness.

Along with the shared national memory in a homogeneous country, there are values that are not much argued about. Sometimes they should be, because much prejudice is hidden this way. When you leave that safe and comfortable place, you do have to re-evaluate a lot of things. I feel as though I have. But there are some things that I will never adjust to. For example, I feel totally alien when the subject of gun control and the right to bear arms comes up. America was founded on the idea of individual rights; but when that idea is taken to such extremes that the common good is forgotten, I despair. There is a tolerance and almost fatalistic acceptance of violence that horrifies me. There are 23,000 homicide victims in this country every year. I cannot understand that good people respond to such violence by buying guns themselves.

One of my problems has to do with language. This will probably surprise my friends, since I talk a lot. I am very comfortable with English, but it isn't mine. The lullabies I sang to my children, and now to my grandchildren, are the songs I went to sleep with when I was a child. Yet when I go home, I find myself searching for words. I find it almost impossible to talk about my job, for example; and every time I am there, I manage to say something that is howlingly funny to everyone else. It heightens my feeling of not really belonging anywhere.

I have changed a lot. The Norway I left does not exist anymore. I know this isn't unique; nobody's home town exists anymore. But for me there is another dimension to it. All this change has taken place in my absence, and somehow that isn't fair. Everybody else changed while I wasn't looking. It feels like I missed the train. When I come back to the United States from a visit to Gjovik, it always seems like a trip from one world to another, and the only connecting link between them is me. Sometimes I feel lost between these worlds. Other times I feel lucky, because I have two countries.

In 1980 my husband and I went to a family reunion. On the day we left Chicago the temperature and humidity were both in the 90s. Thirty hours later we were seated with 150 other descendants of Peder and Laura Husoy on the last inhabited island before the North Sea. It was a rare sunny day, with seagulls and terns floating above shimmering waves; and the air was soft and cool and clean. The tables were covered with white tablecloths, fine china, and bowls of wildflowers.

When Norwegians get together, they often sing, and before the food was served we sang "Millom bakkar og berg utmed havet" ("Between hills and mountains out by the sea"), one of those songs that are part of the Norwegian soul. The words that I had forgotten began to come back, but I was the only one stumbling over them. For everyone else this was a very special day, but a day that was naturally theirs. For me it was a journey back into something I had left. I was suddenly overcome by a sense of past belonging, and I began to weep. Tears streamed down my face. My sister saw what was happening to me, and saved the day by making a joke.

The three days on that tiny island are an unforgettable memory for both my husband and me. We will regret forever that we did not somehow find a way for our college-age children to be there with us. But along with the sense of gratitude that I could be there, I have never forgotten the sudden realization that I had made choices in my life that have made me a stranger to all that anchors my soul. That easy sense of belonging that I once took for granted is lost to me forever.

I do not want this to sound like a wail of self-pity. Although it would not be easy, I could go back to Norway. But I choose to stay in the United States. My children belong here; and fortunately for me, they value their Norwegian heritage and have established their own ties with their relatives. There have been lots of trips back and forth over the years.

I have wonderful friends in the United States, and they make it clear that what is different about me is not a barrier to our friendship. I also enjoy the diversity of American society. I think it would be much more difficult to move into a homogeneous culture. Here everyone is different in some way. The racial and cultural tensions are real, but the United States has done a better job of embracing diversity and turning it into an asset than any other country in the world. In spite of all the problems, there is an awareness that somehow we have to find a way to live together and accept each other.

The 17th of May is Norway's Constitution Day. It is celebrated with music and fireworks, flowers and flags everywhere, parades of children waving flags (no military parades for us), and a great feeling of patriotism and goodwill. Just as Americans abroad feel homesick on Thanksgiving Day, it is a time for Norwegians abroad to reflect. Some years ago on the 17th of May, around our dinner table there were a native American, a Virgin Islander, an Iranian, a German, a Japanese, a Chinese, a Jew, a Moslem, a Catholic, and a "WASP." As I passed the meatballs and other Norwegian dishes, I looked around the table with a sense of gratitude and privilege. If the world is to become a better place, maybe in some sense it has to start in such a way, with people from many different corners of the world celebrating the best in each other.

PART II

Perceptions of College Women

The narratives in this section are by six women college students. At the time they were written in 1992, the students ranged in age from 19 to 26. Of the six, only one was born in the United States; she is of African-American ancestry. The remaining five come from diverse areas of the world: China, Japan, Ecuador, Sri Lanka, and Jamaica.

What the six students have in common, in addition to being female, is that they all have been involved in making transitions from one culture to another. Five out of the six have made international transitions — moving to the United States from other countries — while one has come from a specific U.S. subculture (African-American, metropolitan East Coast) to another (white Anglo-Saxon, small-town Midwestern). Although all six managed to make the transitions successfully, each one experienced difficulty during the initial period of acculturation. Many are now experiencing the beginning of a sense of "cultural homelessness."

All of these women found it hard to make friends. Most reported having to suppress their emotions of loneliness, grief, and anxiety in order to function in the everyday world of the Midwestern college campus. Almost all indicated that they spent the initial months feeling isolated in their rooms with little contact with either the campus or the outside world. There were no support systems in place to help the students through this difficult time.

As these accounts show, an issue of major concern to international and minority students on American college campuses is the extent to which they can take part in campus life without giving up their cultural identity, without becoming assimilated to the host culture. Most seem to prefer an integrative model. They want to learn about the new culture. While they realize that they will take on some of the customs and mannerisms of their new surroundings, they also would like to offer others knowledge about their own culture. And they do not want to compromise their values and beliefs when culture conflicts arise.

A DIVIDED LIFE: WANTING TO BE IN TWO CULTURES AT ONCE

NICOLINA COBO is from Quito, Ecuador. She first came to live in the United States as a high school student when she was 17 years old. After a brief return to her native country, she decided to continue her education in the United States at a college located in the same town where she attended high school. She is currently in her senior year, is majoring in international business and economics, and is a resident assistant in her dormitory. She has won a number of scholarships and currently works part time for an accounting firm.

I remember coming over on the plane all alone, absolutely terrified, to attend high school in the United States, wondering how I had worked up enough courage to do it. When I was growing up in Ecuador, I was always shy and lived a pretty sheltered life. I had traveled to the United States before with my parents and siblings, but I'd never ventured anywhere by myself. Suddenly, at 17, I was on my way to a place I didn't know, a new school, and a new family.

After graduating from high school in Quito, I applied to the Youth for Understanding program to be an exchange student for a year in the United States. My initial motivation for doing this was to learn to speak English fluently. But I also was curious about what it would be like to live in another country for an extended period of time. I had no choice regarding where I would live and go to school. I happened to be placed in a Midwestern town with a white, middle-class family and attended the local high school.

When I first arrived in my new home, I felt rather awkward and uncomfortable. I understood a great deal of what was being said, but it was difficult for me to speak. The training I had in the English language in school in Ecuador lacked emphasis on conversation. I didn't know how to act in the new family setting; I was afraid to take things out of the refrigerator or to turn on the television. It took a long time before I started to feel somewhat comfortable in the house and not so guarded with its occupants.

Even though I lived there for a whole year, I never became totally used to the situation. While other exchange students often call the host parents "mom" and "dad," I was never able to do this and, instead, used my host parents' first names. There were two girls in the family, one exactly my age; but we did not become close friends until recently. While we lived under the same roof, we barely said "hi" and "bye" to each other. My host sisters did their thing, and I did mine.

I had a hard time getting accustomed to my host family's way of life. While they seemed close, they actually spent very little time together. The parents were off to work during the day, and the kids went to school. Then, in the evening, each would frequently have separate activities. Even when everyone was at home, they would eat in different rooms. A daughter might be watching TV and eating her dinner in one room, the father might be listening to the news and eating in another, while the mother might grab something in the kitchen. This was strange for me, since in Ecuador I was used to having supper with the whole family. It was the one time of the day that we all would leave whatever we were doing and come to the table. We would talk about what happened to each one of us in the course of the day. We might discuss some neighborhood matter or talk about politics. This way we kept up on the activities of each family member and stayed close. I accompanied my host family to a few family reunions, but even on these occasions I noticed that people would go off by themselves to do other things rather than stay and talk with their relatives.

At first, it was difficult for me also to be in an American high school. On my first day in school, I was assigned a locker and given a three-number combination for the lock. However, no one explained that you start by turning to the right until you reach the first number. I spent a great deal of time trying to figure it out before I finally gave up and asked someone. I had a terrible time trying to understand what the students were saying. They talked so fast!

Moreover, I was not used to changing classes all the time and to being in class with students from different levels (freshmen, sophomores, juniors). In Ecuador you go through the school system with the same classmates, from first until the twelfth grade. We always stayed in the same classroom with the same group of students, who were roughly of the same age. Only the teachers changed according to subjects taught.

When I started school in the United States, being a senior was another disadvantage for me. The seniors wanted to be together. They had known each other for four years; they were a tightly knit bunch, and it was hard for me to click into their group. So while I met many people and they all seemed friendly, I couldn't get close to anyone.

I managed to form friendships with people I met through the church I attended. A woman I became acquainted with suggested that her sons could pick me up every Sunday and bring me to church. I began to spend time with one of the sons, first going out for Cokes. Eventually we started dating. On the weekends we would go out with his brother, another boy who was living at their house, and their girlfriends. The six of us became a group, and during that year we were inseparable. Sometimes we would do things with other people, but mostly we hung out together. We spent a lot of time at the boys' house, and I developed a warm relationship with the parents. While I don't date the boy anymore, I still feel close to his parents, call his mother almost every week, and visit them frequently.

While being part of a small group of friends and having a steady boyfriend felt good at the time, in retrospect I regret not having done more with other people. I later discovered that there were a number of students at the high school who wanted to invite me to go out with them, but they didn't ask because they knew I was always spending time with that small group.

Toward the end of my year abroad, my host mother suggested that I might consider applying to the college in town. I filled out an application and took the SAT exams. I got an early acceptance and the college was willing to give me some scholarship money. I went back to Ecuador for the summer and considered the possibility of returning for another four years. I discussed with my parents the merits of obtaining an American college diploma, and we agreed that it would be to my advantage. By this time, I had become accustomed to living away from home; and I was pretty confident that I could manage on my own in college.

When I came back in the fall, the transition was no longer difficult for me to make. I knew the language well, I knew people in town, and I even got a roommate who had gone to high school with me. Since most of the first-year students did not know one another, there were no cliques, no existing groups I might have had to break into. We were all starting the same. I no longer felt the disadvantage I had in high school.

To be sure, living on campus in a dormitory is different from living in a family setting. You are more on your own and have greater responsibilities. I also found that I had to spend more time on my studies, since the courses and tests were much more difficult than what I was exposed to in high school.

My foreignness is detectable only when I speak. Since I learned English when I was already out of my childhood, I have a noticeable accent. I have light skin, and therefore look like the majority of students on campus. My verbal difference has not been a problem for me in college. On the contrary, it seems to have helped me make friends. People notice that I speak differently and they ask me where I'm from. Once they know I come from Ecuador, they usually become interested and want to know about my country.

Even though I have adjusted quite well to life on an American college campus, that does not mean that I have given up my own culture or that no problems arise due to my cultural background. For instance, when I first started living in the dorms, I felt very uncomfortable about using communal showers. In Quito, we never showered in school; and also, I suppose, coming from a very Catholic country, I have ingrained in me certain standards of modesty. While I have gotten used to sharing showers, I still don't feel completely comfortable about it.

Another problem for me, especially in my first year of college, was dealing with discussions on topics which in my country would be considered taboo. Sex and sexuality, abortion, incest, women's roles in the church, and women's issues generally are some of the areas that people in my society do not raise or question. So naturally I felt rather awkward when they came up in class or other discussions. Suddenly I was exposed to issues I had never even thought about. People would ask, for example, "Are you pro-life or pro-choice?" In order for me to stay involved in the conversation, I would be forced to think about such issues and to decide for myself what I thought. This was at first very disconcerting because it led me to new ways of looking at things, and sometimes the conclusions I reached on my own did not go along with the unquestioned beliefs of my culture.

I also never thought about women's issues. I always assumed I would get married, my husband would work, and I would stay at home. But now, after being in the United States by myself, I know that I could not do that anymore. I have become independent, and I cannot see myself as just being tied to some male. Rather, I want an education, a job, and I want to be my own person. I am not getting an education in order to stay home, cook, clean, and take care of children. I still want to have a home with husband and children, but I also want a career.

Moreover, it is not realistic these days to assume that one breadwinner can take care of the household. I know such ideas are not popular in my country and that there are fewer professional women there than in the United States. I am aware that there are many obstacles for women pursuing a career in business in the United States, but they are much greater in more traditional Ecuador.

Probably the most difficult thing I have had to deal with as a consequence of having lived for a long time now in another culture is that I don't know where I belong. It's hard because part of me is in Ecuador and part of me is in America. I have been going back and forth every year since 1989; and when I am in one country or the other, I am always missing people and things from the other country. I often feel that I have a divided life, and I wish I could be in both places at once.

While I am still basically the same person who left at 17 on that plane, I also have changed in many ways. Because I came to the United States still in my teens, my ideas were in the process of being formed; and I have learned many things which have made me somewhat different from people at home. My way of looking at things is different, I am definitely more independent and self-confident, and I speak out more. When I go back home, my family and friends notice these changes and they point them out to me.

For instance, when I came home for the summer after my first year at college, my sister took me to a party; and since no one asked me to dance, I just got up and danced by myself. When we came home, my sister said to my mother, "I am not taking her anywhere anymore. She was dancing by herself and embarrassed me. All my friends wanted to know what her problem was." I explained that in the United States it is acceptable to dance by yourself if you go to a party where people are dancing. I added that if I felt like dancing, why should I wait for someone to ask me, rather than just do it and enjoy myself?

A more serious problem I face now when I go back to Ecuador is whether I should speak out on various issues that concern me. For example, if I were to raise such topics as abortion or contraception, some of my friends might feel uncomfortable and assume that, since I have lived in the United States, I would take positions which are opposite to what they believe. And that is not what I want to convey at all. I would like to get them to think about these issues for themselves, the way I have learned to do, and then come to their own conclusions.

In some areas, my views are bound to clash with those of most Ecuadorians. For instance, while I am opposed personally to abortion, I believe that birth control information and contraceptives should be widely available, especially in such a poor country as Ecuador. While some acceptance of this position exists in Ecuador, it goes against the teachings of the Catholic church; and since the vast majority of the population is Catholic, most people would disagree with me. It bothers me that I usually cannot discuss such issues openly with people back home.

My greatest fear right now is about what I will do after finishing college. I ask myself, What if I fall in love with someone in the United States and want to stay? Could I live here permanently? I suppose I could work here for a while after I graduate, but that might be just an extension of college. I am scared that if I go back to Ecuador to live, I am not going to get used to it. But if I stay in the United States, I will never really have a home either. I always look forward to visiting Quito; and once I see my parents, siblings, and friends, I notice that life keeps going on without me and things change. My brother and sister are growing up, my parents are getting older, my friends have gone on to pursue their own goals. We don't have as much in common anymore. I know I can't just go back and resume my life in Ecuador as if nothing happened. I have been profoundly affected by living in another country, and much has changed in Ecuador in the meantime.

Despite this dilemma, I am glad that I have lived in another culture and made the transition on my own. I have learned a great deal, and I am no longer afraid to do things by myself. I am now bilingual, and I would like to learn more languages. I also have become much more interested in the world since I came to the United States. I have met exchange students from several different countries, and now I would like to visit those countries and see how people live in other regions of the globe. I find this possibility immensely exciting.

As a result of going back and forth between Ecuador and the United States during the last three years, I have developed a kind of outsider's perspective on both countries. Rather than accepting conventional or prevalent interpretations of what goes on, I have developed my own views through observations and comparisons. At first I

74

thought that the United States was such a calm and secure country to live in compared to Ecuador, where there is so much poverty and political unrest. Now I realize that living in a small town in the United States, I have been sheltered from its problems.

When I am back in Ecuador, the weight of poverty and political strife is always upon me — there is nowhere to escape from it. Here in the United States, if there are riots in Los Angeles, you can go to the Midwest or the South and be at a safe distance. Moreover, Americans seem to be more optimistic about solving their problems, and, I suppose, with good reason, since they have vast resources to draw on. Ecuador is extremely poor, and so there is not much hope that things can change.

Another observation I have made comparing the two societies is in regard to the class system. Ecuadorian society is rigidly stratified with those of non-native heritage at the top and the native Indian population at the bottom. Class distinctions are visible in terms of where people live, where they go to school, and how they dress.

In the United States it is hard to tell whether someone is from a wealthy, middle class, or poor family just by considering their appearance or how they act. Classes are less visible, since many people have access to such symbols of prestige as education, casual clothes, and cars. There seems to be more homogeneity among the populations, and social class enters people's lives in more subtle ways than in Ecuador.

While I realize that I have been very fortunate to have made my cultural transition to the United States relatively smoothly, I know other international students who have experienced great difficulties. I think what would be very helpful to new students who come to campus straight from another country, region, or cultural setting is to have people their own age to talk to about what they are experiencing. A peer support group, made up of international and minority students, could ease a great deal of the initial uncertainty and fear of new students who are culturally different.

TRYING TO UNDERSTAND: A SRI LANKAN IN AN AMERICAN COLLEGE

RIKA FRANKE came to the United States to attend college in 1991 at the age of 25 from Colombo, Sri Lanka, after having worked for four years in advertising layout, design, and copywriting. She chose to attend a small, Midwestern college because she had worked with one of its alumni, who recommended it. Currently completing her undergraduate major in journalism, she plans graduate study in human rights law.

When I lived at home in Sri Lanka, before I ever came to the United States, I didn't picture that life was going to be so provincial. I have lived all my life in a city. When I traveled to Europe, I traveled mostly in the cities; and so I based my image of America on that. From what I had seen in Europe, I assumed it would be like that. I never thought about the countryside. I never even imagined this isolated little place in the middle of cornfields, with no public transportation, nothing to do, no cultural stimulation as far as I was concerned.

That was my initial reaction. The West has always been culturally developed and technologically advanced, so I naturally imagined there would be conveniences like transportation. I never thought I would be without a means of getting around.

One thing that made the transition easier for me than for some other international students is that I speak English. I didn't have to learn the language. My parents grew up in a British colony, so there are inevitably certain Western values that they acquired unconsciously, and that I absorbed from them.

It also helped that many members of my mother's and father's families lived in other countries, so I had been exposed to many cultures and cultural differences. I had been to England, Germany, Austria, Belgium, Holland, France, Italy, Switzerland, and Japan. I believe that all this prepared me to some extent for going to the United States for an extended period.

Actually, I don't know the differences between my Western values and experiences and my Asian values and experiences. I don't distinguish between them because they are all part of me. I grew up reading English books; I don't know the fables that a child who grows up in my country should know. I didn't grow up reading native stories. I have spoken English all my life; I speak it much more than my native language. On coming to the United States, I found that a lot of the stories, the books, even the old music, were already very much part of my life. People expect me to have had Sri Lankan cultural experiences, but I can't identify them. Of course, I have had different cultural experiences; but for the major part of my life, I've lived with my parents. Much of what they've known is part of me, part of my cultural background. I can't separate out the Asian from the Western because they've been blended in me.

I had thought I was somewhat prepared for moving to the United States, but it turned out not to be so. I think what handicapped me was my dependence on my family. I had very close bonds with my parents and siblings. I had traveled outside my country, but I hadn't been away from them for long. For example, I always knew I was going back to them after a three-month vacation. But leaving for a much longer period and then coming into an empty dormitory room were awful. I arrived before the other students, since college wasn't in session yet; and I was just there, alone, in a sparsely furnished room.

My assigned roommate, a Lebanese girl, wasn't scheduled to come for a month. In fact, she never arrived. So I got another roommate, but not until the following month. For a month I had the room to myself. It was difficult, but I wonder if I wasn't actually fortunate, because I enjoy being alone. Going into a room and closing the door meant that I had my privacy. If I wanted to interact and socialize, I could always go out of my room and meet people. So in a way, it was good; but initially, it was not easy.

The most alien experience for me was living in a dorm. I had my own room at home. Guests at home were given their own room and bath. Being among a group of strangers and then having to share bath facilities with them was difficult for me.

In a way I'm glad I didn't have a roommate initially, because it would have been more of a culture shock to try to adjust to a new person with different views and different ways of looking at things. Living alone allowed me to adjust for a while from a distance, and then I didn't mind it so much.

I found it hard to get used to my new surroundings. For one thing, I didn't expect the intense heat. I was expecting it to be cold, or at least cool. I had no air conditioning, and I was sweating it out until one of the students I met gave me an electric fan.

Initially, I was not comfortable with the students in my dorm. I think that had a lot to do with my age, as well. I was 25 when I arrived. I couldn't relate to what they found funny. For example, whenever someone said something wrong or did something wrong – made a language mistake, or dropped something, or did something that was embarrassing to themselves – students would laugh at them. We don't do that at home.

If a person fell or someone we didn't know well dipped her sleeve in her soup, we wouldn't laugh at her. Only if we knew a person well, would we tease her. If we didn't know the person, we would go on as if nothing had happened and either help her clean up or ask if she was all right and then carry on. Here I found that people tended to dwell on the embarrassment. Their humor seemed juvenile.

On reflection, I think that it was a cultural difference, and not merely a difference in maturity level. At home we wouldn't want to embarrass the other person. I think now, after having been in the United States for a while, that the purpose of the laughter is to ease the embarrassment on the other person's part. In my culture we behave differently, perhaps for the same reason: a different cultural approach to the same problem.

I think people in Sri Lanka are much more friendly, or perhaps more sincere in friendship. Maybe I'm being partial. I would think that if people in my country made an effort to help someone who is a stranger, it would be done because they wanted to do it, and it would be a continued thing. It wouldn't be just an initial reaction, followed by the thought, "Okay, I've done my bit now." In the United States, what appears to be initial friendliness toward or initial interest in the newcomer doesn't seem to continue.

Americans appear to be very friendly at first meeting, overly so in fact; but they have difficulty maintaining this friendliness in subsequent encounters. In many other cultures, including my own, people are polite at first and then, as they get to know the person better, they become friendlier and warmer. Non-Americans are frequently thrown off by Americans' initial friendliness. They expect close friendship to ensue; and when it does not, they feel confused. People appeared more friendly at first than I am used to, but I felt that they were superficially so. Upon first meeting someone, I would be cordial, not overly-friendly. Perhaps I even appeared unfriendly by comparison. Americans seemed overly-friendly; but the next time I saw them, they either didn't see me or didn't know me. That was a big difficulty.

Consequently, when I first arrived on campus, I felt somewhat welcome, but not especially so. I was just one of a big group of freshmen; but perhaps at that point I was disoriented and upset, and I wanted and needed more than they could give.

To me, friends are people you've known for five or six years or more. I don't mean merely the time you've known them, but what you've built with them. In a new country you can't make friends in your first semester, or even in your second semester. You can't call them "acquaintances" either; I wish there were an intermediate term.

I didn't even think of the difficulty of finding friends before I came. I think I took friendship for granted, because I'd lived at home all my life and I have a group of friends that I've grown up with. I tended to take that friendship base for granted. At home I didn't need to look for groups to participate in. They were there for me. One either opted to do something with one's friends or opted out. That was the choice, not whether to go looking for people with whom to do things. I never even imagined that I would have to make new friends or find people to do things with.

Since I hadn't actively made an effort to make friends for a long time, I didn't do it when I came to the United States. Living in the dorm helped because the students all lived in the same environment. We were brought into contact with the same people, socialized and interacted with each other. So in that way, I think, we eventually made friends without looking for them.

If I could, I would have wanted to befriend someone of my own culture and, if that weren't possible or available, one person whom I could fall back on, so to speak.

I did find some support at the college. One particular person has been a great source of support both in school and outside. She's not of my own cultural background. She's American and she has helped me a great deal. I met her when we both worked in the same area of the college. She had a Sri Lankan student living with her before, so I knew there was some sort of empathy and understanding. But I found it difficult to open myself up. In a new country, you don't know the people. You can't just go up to them and pour your heart out. But I appreciated that support. It isn't necessary to talk with a person to sense her support, and sometimes it helps just to know that someone is there.

The college provided us with an orientation program. Many people said, "You can come to me with anything." I know it sounds awful, but I didn't trust them, because it was their job to tell me that. I wanted to find someone who was genuinely concerned with my predicament, and you can't expect that, really. The college, I think, did provide quite a bit. For instance, one of the counselors always told us that we could speak to him about anything. There is also the Trust group, a student support group; but I could not relate to these people. I didn't even try. I didn't want to.

At first, everything seemed to be a facade. Maybe groups like that are formed in a conscious and positive effort to help people, the groups like sororities and the Trust group. However, to me, they seemed just to be groups with nothing, really, to offer, aside from the "group-ness."

In Sri Lanka we aren't encouraged to be excessively sentimental or to express our feelings or to be overly emotional. I didn't sit down to have lunch with my friends or family and discuss my deep feelings, ever. I find it difficult to approach someone and to pour out my heart.

Still, I find it difficult not having that base of people, that ready-made band of friends and family around. Everything is possible when that's there for you. It's security. I still haven't been able to adjust to that, to the lack of that security and warmth.

I miss my family. From what I've heard from classmates, there are significant differences between families in the United States and families in Sri Lanka. I personally haven't found very many differences, since I haven't had very much experience — I've just lived with one American family. (After living in the dormitory for a semester, I went to live with the family of a member of the college staff.) The family I live with is a very close-knit one; but from what I gather, the American family unit doesn't seem as special as it is in Sri Lanka. For instance, at home we make an attempt to eat together. Even if we don't, we sit together at the table and discuss things.

Families at home seem more supportive; they encourage more dependence by the children on the parents and on the family unit. I don't know whether that's good or bad. In my case it was a handicap, because that was a big part of why I found it difficult to be away from home. Leaving the support that I had all my life — that was a big break with the past.

I've found many cultural differences in making the transition to student life in the United States. In the first semester, the transition

81

was very difficult for me. I occupied myself by thinking only about my studies, nothing else. It was definitely difficult for all the reasons I mentioned earlier and all the differences and the fears — you feel so insecure because there is no one you can go to.

Another thing I've noticed is the abrasive quality of people. I have been quite taken aback at times. People seemed rude. At home I would observe certain boundaries. To me, it was courtesy. Students here didn't seem to have that. I have discussed this with many people; and it seems that it may be because parents here don't want to inhibit their children, so they socialize them to be individualistic and assertive. As a result, they become self-involved. Maybe that is one of the reasons.

Perhaps it's a difference in what is considered courtesy. If someone else is speaking to another person, I wouldn't interrupt. I would make my presence felt so the other person knew I would like to speak, unless I was in a hurry; then I would say, "Excuse me." When two people are talking in a corridor, I don't walk in between them, as students here do. I know this sounds very minor, trivial; but these are cultural differences I've observed.

At home if I come into the living room and my parents are talking, I don't just walk in and turn the TV on. I say, "Do you mind if I turn it on? I have a program I want to watch." Even if it's my home, and I know it's home and I'm comfortable there, I would still say that.

Another difference I've noticed is an attitude of self-interest on the students' part. For instance, at home if someone came to me with a problem, not a problem a stranger would find too difficult or too great, I would make an effort to help. But I don't think people here do that. It's as if they always put themselves first; and anything that doesn't contribute to the furthering of themselves or anything that is time-consuming, they choose not to spend time on. Maybe they feel that you should find out for yourself, learn by trial and error. It seems that here people would prefer you to learn by yourself, rather than provide help. I feel that the American students I've encountered are not likely to put themselves out or to inconvenience themselves in order to help another person.

Another difference between the two cultures is in the teacher-student relationships. No respect is required of the students toward each other or toward the professor. In my country elders are respected. Even if what an older person says isn't exactly what you believe in or isn't your opinion, you don't openly disagree. In a very subtle manner, it is conveyed; but you always show a certain amount of deference, especially to much-older people.

Here, I think that respect is not shown. Even if the person that the students are speaking with is very much older, they go ahead and say what they think. In my country a student would never call a professor by his or her first name. We are more formal. The way one addresses people and the language one uses among people who are very much older is different from the way one would talk with one's friends. The lack of deference to elders struck me, especially initially, as rudeness; that may be another cultural difference.

From my classroom experience, I can cite an instance of a difficulty American students seem to have in exploring certain topics. In a general education class, where a lot of ideas are discussed with respect to literature, I found that students had difficulty entertaining ideas and values that differed from theirs, especially ones that questioned religious belief or implied that there were beliefs other than the ones that they held, valued beliefs that other people held.

Also, students found it difficult to handle discussion about literature in which there was sexual innuendo. In a literature class, of course, you have to discuss every possible angle in a piece of writing. I felt that the students were inhibited. They seemed to have an instant shut-off point. It should have been an objective discussion of what was in the text or the interpretation of what might be in the text. But when it came to the sexual interpretation, it became almost a personal thing. I found that the students couldn't discuss it. Instead, they denied that any such interpretation was possible. A lot of moralizing resulted. They would say that people shouldn't do this or that. If a literary character did something that went against the students' own values, there would be hostility toward the character.

Because I was older than they were, it might have been a difference in maturity. But I saw a discussion of sex in literature as just an exchange of ideas. To American students, it was something much more personal. That's what led me to believe that they've led sheltered lives. They haven't been exposed to much. Definitely at home, we're exposed to much more international news; and we discuss fairly sensitive topics, I would say, with no qualms about it.

The students I've met haven't been exposed to poverty, pain, suffering, or having to do without. At home, it's around us; and so, for instance, we would never throw food away. That's nothing here in this country. I also found that most people don't appear to be interested in world affairs. I guess it is because they get a lot of their news from the TV, which is limited in its scope, whereas we get most of our news from newspapers.

I'm not sure if this is a cultural difference or merely a matter of abundance, but I try not to let material things become too important to me. I don't want to get too obsessed by possessions. Many people in the United States seem consumed by material things. I don't believe material things are important. Sri Lanka is a poor country, and we don't have nearly as much as people do in the United States. Sri Lankans don't have the choices Americans have. I think, given the chance, people in Sri Lanka might become inclined to want more things. I, myself, wouldn't want to have the money and think, "Well, I have the money and now I can have anything I want." I also don't want to move away from nature.

I feel that Americans are overly materialistic and convenience-oriented. With every fast food, convenience food, plastic cup, and throwaway, Americans are moving farther and farther from the real and natural things in life. I am not a Buddhist, but Sri Lanka is heavily influenced by Buddhism. Buddhism encourages moderation. Assuming that materialism is excessive, I suppose that would be a cultural difference between my culture and American culture.

I've found some small differences in the roles of women in the two cultures. I think the women students are more assertive in the United States than they would be in Sri Lanka. However, the group of people who go to universities at home are more assertive, too, including women. Perhaps assertiveness is related to levels of education. But on the whole, although there is much talk of feminism in America, I don't think the roles of women here and at home are very different.

There are things I've derived from my cultural background that I don't want to change. There are cultural differences that I don't want to accommodate, although in some ways I have changed since I arrived in the United States. I was a bit more timid when I came. Perhaps not timid, but quieter. I tend to express myself more now only because I have to, especially if I want anyone here to know me as an individual.

At home, with people who have lived around me for a long time, I do things without thinking because I know how people are going to interpret my behavior. But here there's a lot of misinterpretation, and then I have to go back and explain. For example, it seems that people here encourage opinions; and the opinions have to be spoken. If you don't express an opinion, it means you are weak and you don't have opinions. In Sri Lanka, that isn't required very often.

At home, just because you don't voice your opinion doesn't mean you don't have one. It's just that you choose not to voice it. I find this very difficult, because people think, "Oh, she's Asian so she's timid." If I don't agree with something, I just don't go along with it. I don't have to stand on a podium and say, "I don't think so." It doesn't necessarily do much to be vociferous about something. If I choose to let an opinion I don't agree with go by, it's not because I'm timid; it's because I don't see any point in retorting. To me sometimes it's a waste of time. I understand someone may have a different point of view, and they are entitled to it; but I really don't want to waste my time trying to change it. It's not that important to me. Here, that's considered almost sacrilegious. You have to take a stand. As a consequence, if I don't voice my opinions, people misunderstand me.

In the United States, people seem to like a lot of visibility and they like to put others into types, classes, or boxes. So, naturally, if you don't talk, don't say much, don't make friends, you go into one box. People don't accept you for what you are. There's so much talk of individualism, but what people do is to try to put you into a specific group, a category: a geek, a yuppie, etc.

There are other small cultural differences, as well, that I've noticed. For instance, in the United States, people don't greet each other with kisses. At home they do, especially with friends and family. When my brother and I see each other, before we say anything, we give each other a hug and kiss on both cheeks. It's a very nice custom that I don't see here, and an interesting cultural difference. I miss it.

Despite my frustrations, there are things I have gained in making this cross-cultural transition. I would say I have become much stronger. You have to be. I think that's one of the major points, the good points of my transition. Another is academic. I have gained more confidence, seeing my work, seeing the results after going through my studies. It makes me feel worthwhile. The educational part of this transition has enriched me.

I'm glad I made this transition because I think it has not only made me a stronger person but it has also given me a lot of confidence in what I can do. I'm not afraid anymore to just go out and do things because I feel I want to, to be adventurous and do something that I really believe in, even if no one is behind me. I have enough faith in myself to do that.

Some of the very things I initially found different and difficult I now appreciate. The fact that people in the U.S. culture encourage you to be independent and individualistic helps people to mature more quickly.

In some ways, this experience will make it difficult to go back to Sri Lanka. I think that I would be very impatient with the failures of the system at home because I find that the infrastructure in the United States makes living convenient: the fact that people in the United States view work in relation to time, that services work efficiently, the fact that people take their responsibilities very seriously. The very things I liked at home I might dislike now: the lackadaisical manner, the easy-going life that I used to love. I am afraid that I will be impatient with it now.

I've adopted subtle attitudes and behaviors that are American, and I'm probably not aware of them. I can't tell anymore if I recognize cultural differences, because the lines have blurred. Things that seemed alien at first now seem familiar. Things are so much better for me now than when I first came, and I'm quite happy and feel secure. I don't know, when I go back, if I will fit anymore and feel at home in my own culture. Ironically, my adjustment to this culture has hidden costs.

I hope that there aren't other costs. I hope my family is essentially the same when I go back and that my relationships remain the same. Of course, they will be different. I have changed, and my friends will have changed also. I hope there won't be greater costs.

There are still things that I miss. I miss the freedom to be able to go places, to get away, to travel, to find public transportation. I also miss my family a lot. I miss the sea, because on a hot day you can always go out and lie in the sun or swim in the sea. I miss the sound of the sea. I miss that a lot.

I miss the food.

I miss the sun.

LEARNING TO VALUE
ONE'S HERITAGE

XING CHUN ZHENG came to the United States in 1990 from the People's Republic of China, where she had been a university student at the time of the Pro-democracy Movement, which was crushed in 1989. She spent a year attending a college in Iowa and then moved, entering a college in Indiana in 1991 at the age of 20. In the fall of 1993, she studied at a university in Nancy, France, and plans to pursue a graduate degree in computer science after completing her bachelor's degree.

I don't expect many people in the United States to be able to pronounce my name correctly, so I ask people to call me Alex. When I first arrived in the United States, the woman I stayed with could not say my name. She suggested that I choose an American name for myself. I had always liked the Russian name Alexander; and so we both decided that she would call me "Alex," and it has stuck.

I'm from a very densely populated city of 12 million people, Shanghai, in the People's Republic of China. Coming to the United States to a small-town Midwestern college is really a big change for me. Since I already had almost 13 years of education back in my country, Chinese culture is deeply rooted in my mind.

I have an uncle who lives in Iowa, and I went there when I first came to the United States. My transition to Iowa was very peaceful because people in the town I lived in study meditation and Eastern cultures. I spent the summer there, and then went to a college nearby for a year before moving to Indiana.

In Iowa I made a lot of friends. Unfortunately, almost every one of them was a foreigner. Foreigners are easier to get along with, in my experience. We are looking for the same thing, because we are all interested in other cultures. We are all the same type of person. We call ourselves "international persons," and we are probably atypical in our own countries as well.

The first time I really experienced culture shock was when I began school in Iowa. It's so different back in my country from the United States. We have much more discipline. My country reveres Confucius. We are taught to respect elders and to respect teachers. The first week in my American college classroom, I heard a student say "bullshit" to the teacher. I was really shocked. The teacher was so calm; she still smiled and went on teaching.

People treat teachers with greater respect in my culture. Knowledge is very highly valued. Sometimes I think students in the U.S. college classroom are kind of rude. They interrupt the professor to ask questions or to state their disagreement. In one class I witnessed a student interrupt the teacher in the middle of a sentence to disagree, and he actually began to speak with an expression of anger. Even students' tones of voice convey disrespect sometimes. Once, a student who didn't see something that the teacher had referred to in a text told the teacher that it wasn't there, instead of asking where it was. I can ask the teachers questions; but I say, "Excuse me." At least I try to be polite, but I see students who are very rude. In China, in our schools and universities, you never see this kind of rudeness.

In elementary school in China, all the kids are afraid of the teacher. If your parents can't control you, they say, "I'll tell your teacher." No child would do anything bad when threatened like this because children are so afraid of their teachers.

I remember the first time I went to elementary school. I was six years old, and the teacher told us we should be unselfish. Two people would share a desk and take as little space as possible. So I always wrote in a corner. After a semester, I couldn't write straight. Then, the teacher noticed that I was writing in this awkward way. In my culture, it is better not to have too much individuality, so my teacher said, "Why don't you write like other students? You should keep your notebook straight." But I couldn't do that anymore. At quiz time, the teacher always stood behind me and asked me to keep my notebook straight; and I would have to write very, very slowly because I was not accustomed to holding the notebook that way.

I spent two years at Fu Dan University in Shanghai; but in study time, it only amounted to one semester. That's not because I skipped class for a year-and-a-half but in large part because of the Prodemocracy Movement. After my first semester, there was a student strike; and later, when classes resumed, I had difficulty changing my major. I thought then that I would like to study abroad. In China, it is very difficult to be admitted to a university, and the rules for remaining in the university are very strict. If you want to study abroad, you must quit in order to do it; and if you don't return within one year, you must take the entrance exam all over again and risk not being admitted. Once I applied for a visa to study in the United States, I had to withdraw from the university.

I think I am more serious about studying than most students I've met at the two Midwestern schools I've attended. Maybe this is because I'm from very strict Chinese schools. Middle school, high school, and university were all very strict. In my Confucian culture, people view education as Jewish people do; they place it in the most important position. It's better to be a university professor and to earn $40,000 per year than to be a businessman and earn $200,000 per year. We think it's more pure. The relative prestige of careers in my society is different from what it is here. We think seeking knowledge is something noble.

In the United States, graduate school and undergraduate school seem very different. I have talked with graduate students whom I found to be very mature. In colleges in the Midwest, I think undergraduate students are immature. They like to talk about things like movie stars. In China, at a university, people like to talk about politics or literature or life. If you talk about these things to American students, they think you are nuts. Still, I like it here very much. At the college where I am now enrolled, I feel some students are very good. From my conversations with them, I know they're eager to learn and they like to think. But in the other Midwestern college I attended before coming here, people didn't like to think, and they were not very friendly toward foreigners.

I like the teachers at the college where I'm presently enrolled. The major reason I feel very comfortable is that almost every one of my professors is very helpful. They are very understanding, open-minded, and close to their students.

My country is like a pyramid. Only the very top few people can go to the university. Most of those people would like to come to America because of the freedom here; you have more opportunity to develop your potential. Most of the people from my country who come to the United States are well educated. Of course, America also is like a pyramid. The difference between the U.S. pyramid and the Chinese pyramid is that if you go to a university in China, that means you've already been pre-selected. If you are in a Chinese university, all your life you've been communicating with mostly educated people and with people similar to you. They can talk with you intellectually. But here in the United States, I noticed that many different people can go to a college or university, even some who can't do basic math very well. In my society, we have one billion people and, at the most, one million would ever go to universities.

All the people in China are supposed to have equal opportunity to be educated. I'm from a big city, and fortunately I'm from a very open-minded family. My family encouraged me to be whatever I wanted to be. But that is not always true. Usually, in the city or in an educated family, I see Chinese women basically being stronger than Chinese men. In China, women traditionally have been suppressed. Because of the cultural restrictions, women have developed emotional and mental strength.

On the other hand, men have been somewhat elevated all their lives. Traditionally, sons are more valued than daughters in many families. So after liberation, when the Communist Party imposed equality between women and men, women who were just as smart or competent as men had that extra emotional and mental strength to draw upon. I think that women make cultural transitions more easily than men for the same reason.

A Chinese woman in the city is brought up to compete with men, but it is very different in the countryside. When I was in my first year at the university, I went on a trip with a friend to the western part of China. The basic reason for the trip was a kind of adventure. We wanted to learn about the "real" China, and so we went to visit a village. In the village people didn't encourage the children to receive much education because they thought, "What's the use of books. You can't eat them; you can't produce any food from them." Especially for girls, the villagers think education is less important. We visited a family in the village with a very pretty 16-year-old daughter. She had attended school for only two years; and when we showed her some books, she seemed fascinated. She told us how much she wanted to go to school; but her family didn't have money to send her, so she had to work in the fields. It was very sad. Her future is to marry and to live this way for the rest of her life.

I hoped to make many friends in college, but at my present college I haven't made many friends. One reason is lack of time. I work and study a lot, so I don't have much chance to get to know people. I have conversations with American students; but to know them really well takes time, and I still feel that's kind of hard.

One problem is topics of conversation. The girls like to talk about boys all the time. I'm not interested because I feel that what they talk about is superficial. In my culture we only talk about these things when we become good friends, not just acquaintances. Maybe I'm a very private person, but this is probably a cultural difference.

In conversations with American students, we seem to lack common topics. A lot of people at the college only stay in their own geographic area. That's very different from me. I like to go places and to learn about different people and their cultures. The Midwestern students I have met don't seem to. They don't know much about me, and sometimes I feel they are indifferent to my culture. They seem interested in me for a few minutes, and then the temperature goes down. Of course, I've found some people I can talk to; but the number of friends I have made is small, probably because I don't have much contact with the students, not deep contact.

I thought I couldn't get along with American young people very well, but a trip to my friend's college in another state changed my mind. I made many friends at this other college. We talked about many interesting things — about music, travel, life, everything. I think that it's not helpful to generalize about "students in America." I've seen only a small portion of America's students, and there are regional differences in this country.

I think friendship is something very serious. There's a difference between an acquaintance and a friend. With some people you know the friendship will last for a lifetime. I found at some American colleges it is very easy for people to say "hello." You meet a person who is very friendly toward you. The next day, that person may totally ignore you. In my country people don't become so close at first. People in China are more reserved. We are not taught to go to others; we expect people to come to us. I believe that we Chinese need to be more sociable. People from Eastern cultures are more shy, and it doesn't hurt to be more open to people. However, I don't understand friendliness that disappears after the first meeting.

Since I came to the United States, I've noticed many differences between American and Chinese culture. I didn't recognize them much at first; but the longer I've been in America, the more I've felt them. One difference is the idea of independence. When I was in China, I had the notion that every American was very independent; but after I came here I noticed that to gain this independence, one has to sacrifice a lot of things. I stayed for a time with a woman in Iowa who said she had to be divorced to be independent. That was her feeling about being married. I don't think women in China think about independence in this way.

One of the most important differences between Chinese and American cultures is in male-female relationships. People here seem to take these relationships much more casually than in my culture. I remember watching a comedy in which a Japanese woman said, "In our culture if I say I like you, that means I love you and I want to marry you." But here, "I love you" can mean "Please take me to the airport."

I've noticed a very big difference in dating. In my culture you only date people whom you like very much. Here, first you date a person, then you decide whether you like him or not. It's very different. This is something that is hard for me to adapt to. In my culture a date is still boyfriend-girlfriend stuff, but in America, I understand that it's just simply that two people go out and it probably means nothing, though you call it a "date." In my culture, if you call it a "date," it means something serious.

In China when people become close, it is more spiritual. People really love each other and commit to each other. I think generally people in my country give these types of relationships more weight. But here it's easy for people to say, "I love you," and easy for them to have a sexual relationship. Then when everything is finished, they say, "I don't love you anymore." In my country if two people love one another, the couple should be one entity. It's a more emotional link between people than what I see in the United States.

I experienced another cultural surprise when I was on a visit to Colorado. My friends, two American boys and two girls, and I went for a hike up a mountain. My friend and I and one American boy were the only ones who made it to the top of the mountain. Then, as we were coming down, it began to rain. The American boy began to take his raincoat out of his backpack, and I was expecting him to ask me to take his raincoat, as one would in my culture. But he put his raincoat over his head and said, "You should walk faster. You don't have a raincoat, and you'll get pneumonia."

In America you have to advertise yourself as good, for then people will recognize that you are good. In my culture if people think you are good, you must be very humble and modest and say, "Oh, no. I'm not very good." You have to wait until other people say you are good, or they consider you very cocky or ostentatious. In China, people think that if you have a big mouth, you don't have much inside. In the United States you've got to have a big mouth so you can promote yourself.

When I left China I was not very sad; but the longer I stay in the United States, the more I feel I'm affiliated to my own culture and country. When I first came over, I was not very tradition-minded. Even my American friend in China said I was just like an American girl. But I don't think he knew me very well. I think that, compared to other people, I was open-minded at that time. I didn't know very much about my own culture. I had read a lot of Western novels from the time I was in elementary school, so I really appreciated Western values. After I came to the United States, my uncle, who is a very traditional Chinese, taught me a lot about Confucianism and Taoism. I stayed with him for a year, and I learned more than I had in all my previous life. It was wonderful. It made some things about my own culture far more valuable to me. I've concluded that I don't want to become just part of the "melting pot" and lose my identity. I want to keep some things for myself as a Chinese.

I learned about America before I came, but I don't think I really knew American culture very well. I had a very biased view. I thought the whole country was all the same. But now I know that people from different parts of the country are different. There are regional and subcultural differences.

When I came here, my beliefs were somewhat American. Americans have some basic principles, like freedom and individuality. That was what I was seeking. I think at that time I was very idealistic. My generation hadn't received much basic, traditional education in Chinese culture; so as Western influences came to our society, most of the young people craved Western culture instead of looking back to our own culture.

I want to make myself clearer. When I came here from my country, I was 19 years old and, like most of my friends, I had an American dream. From what we saw on TV, we got a false image of what America was like. We came over here full of hope, and then we saw the reality. It was not bad, but it was not as good as we had imagined. In my country, we appreciate Western culture instead of valuing our own culture. The longer I am away from my country, the more I look back to and am attracted to my own culture.

One thing that is very good about America is that you become more responsible for yourself. In my culture I was taken care of by my parents. I didn't need to worry about anything. Probably if I had graduated from my Chinese university, I would have had a ready-made job. Most likely my parents or relatives would have helped me to get a good job. The family wants to take care of you all the time. I remember when I first went to the university in China, my mom would make the bed for me and do all those kinds of things. Here, since I am alone, I am obliged to be mature, to live by myself, and to take care of myself. I think it's very good to be responsible. I don't think I'm a child anymore.

I had never worked in my country, but I've worked quite a bit in this country. The first time I worked, I really felt changed. I needed to walk for 25 minutes to get to work. Before I accepted the job, I called my uncle, saying, "How will I get to my job?" "You can walk," he answered. How could I walk? It was winter, and I was very uncomfortable. But after I did this, I felt that anything was possible as long as I was willing to do it. I think that's a very good thing about America.

One thing that I found shattering in the United States is the discrimination against people who are different. Some people discriminate against black people, who seem different and alien to them. They don't understand that people are basically all the same. Actually, when you know more about people in the world, you know that everybody is the same deep down inside. I'm proud of being a Chinese, but I've met Chinese who are ashamed that they are Chinese because of American attitudes. A lot of Americans limit their understanding of the Chinese to Chinese food. That's it: Chinese means Chinese food. In my country, of course, we don't care that much about Chinese food because we eat Chinese food all the time. But Americans don't know much about Chinese culture. We have 5,000 years of history and culture. This is far more important than Chinese food, and it's what I would want Americans to know about China.

A lot of countries have very rich cultures, but they are not very well-developed economically. Thus, Americans seem to ignore their cultures. American ideas about Communism have made many Americans believe that everything in China was bad. In colleges, they should ask international students to explain their cultures so that American students could learn more about other cultures.

I think there are costs associated with making a cultural transition. Being away from my parents, my family, and all my friends has been very difficult. I spent nearly two years at the university in China with my friends. They are all working or in graduate school now. All of us who came to America are still in school. I don't know when I will finish, because I want to go on to graduate school as well. The time I've lost is a cost, too.

I also gave up security. Here I have to take care of myself. There were times after I came to the United States when I didn't have a place to live. I felt very insecure. I had never worried about where

I would live until I came to America. My home is not here. When I went to school in Iowa, during vacations when the dorms closed, I could always go back to my uncle's place. At my present college it is different. When the dorms close, I have to find a place to live until they reopen.

I think there are also advantages to having made this cross-cultural transition. I learned one thing that is very good. I have become very bold. In the classroom in my country, we would never be able to talk. If you wanted to talk, you'd have to raise your hand until the teacher addressed you, and that would only be in very rare cases. Usually you would ask questions only about what the teacher lectured on. If you had other questions, you had to wait until the class was over and then you'd ask the teacher.

During the first year I was in America, I always waited until class was finished. Then I would say to the professor, "May I ask you some questions?" Now, I think I am like American students, always interrupting and saying, "What do you think about this?" In my culture, we are supposed to be very obedient and just listen. In China, they say you come to the classroom to learn and to listen, not to talk. In the United States you come to talk. It's very different.

I've learned a great deal. I have a new appreciation for other cultures, and I appreciate my own more. I always am studying and working. I've changed a lot. But as long as I stick to my most serious values and principles, it's all beneficial for me. And I don't think I will change my values, because I still think that is a very serious, important thing.

MOST DIFFICULT BUT MOST VALUABLE EXPERIENCE

━━━━━━━━━━━━━━━━━━━━━━━━━━━━━━━━━━━━

YUKO KANDA comes from Kuji, Japan, where she lived the first 18 years of her life. She came to the United States as a student, spending the first three months in an English-as-a-Second Language (ESL) program, and then enrolled in a small, private, liberal arts college in the Midwest. She currently is a senior majoring in economics and is interested in learning several languages, including Lithuanian. As the first student representative from her city to its sister city in Indiana, she has taken every opportunity to introduce Japanese culture to Americans.

Coming to the United States by myself without really knowing the language or anyone here was a scary prospect, even though I had wanted to do it for a while before I was able to leave Japan. When I was still in high school in Kuji, I applied to a short-term exchange program provided by the prefecture, hoping to spend a summer in the United States. The competition for such exchange opportunities was great, and I was not chosen. When I was in my last year of high school, my teachers, who knew I wanted very much to go to America, told me that Kuji was looking for someone to send to the college that was located in its sister city. I applied and this time was selected.

The first transition I made from Japan to the United States involved spending three months in an English Language Center on the campus of a college that was located in a large Midwestern city. Even though I had studied English in Japan, I was far from proficient in the language. The college I was going to attend suggested that I take the ESL course. Along with 70 other students from many countries, including China, Panama, Turkey, France, Japan, and others, I lived in a dormitory and studied English. This was a wonderful experience for me. While I missed my home and family, all the people with whom I was studying were in the same situation. Even though we did not speak English very well, we did not have much trouble understanding each other and were able to communicate better and better the more English we learned. There were several Japanese students; and after a whole day of struggling in English, I could find respite by talking with them in my native language.

After three months of living in close quarters and learning from one another about our countries, many of us became good friends. It was not easy to say good-bye. We promised to write and to visit each other in our home countries. If I am to keep my promises, in the future I shall have to travel to Korea, China, Switzerland, Brazil, and Germany.

After the language school, we all went our separate ways, most attending colleges and universities within the state or surrounding ones. I have kept in touch with several of the students who located not too far from my college, and we have communicated largely by telephone. I was very sad when we had to part, but I also looked forward to starting classes at the college and putting my newly acquired knowledge of English into practice.

I arrived on campus just in time to audit summer school. This was not the best time to begin college, as most people are gone and activities are down to minimum. While the staff and my African-American roommate were friendly, they didn't pay all that much attention to me. I felt somewhat let down and lonely. After the intense experience of the Language School, I expected more of the same at the college. Also, I think I was anticipating some sort of a grand welcome, the kind of reception people of my country give to guests from abroad. If a foreign student were to come to my school in Kuji, we all would go out of our way to pay attention to him or her and make sure that this person would be well taken care of. It became clear to me that if I wanted or needed something here, I would have to ask. This was not easy because I tend to be shy, and I still did not feel very confident about my English.

Those first few months were very hard for me. I was left alone a lot of the time, I missed my family and friends, and I didn't have anyone in whom I could confide. I think that even if there were such a person, I might not have had the ability to express my feelings. I also found that students and faculty seemed to have difficulty comprehending my English, and I struggled very hard to make myself understood.

The way I dealt with my situation during those first few months was to cut off as much of my emotions as I could. In Japan it is quite common not to express one's feelings, not to talk about oneself. I drew on this cultural reserve and tried to be strong. I tried not to think about the emotional turmoil that was inside me and instead concentrated on academic work. Once the regular semester began, I spent most of my time away from classes in my room, studying. As a result, my view became very myopic.

I did not know what was happening in the world, as I didn't read newspapers or watch news on television. And I had no idea of what was happening on the campus as well, since I did not belong to any groups or attend any of the activities. All of this was very different from what I had been used to in Japan. I always watched the news and read newspapers and magazines to be well-informed. I took pride in knowing what was happening in the world around me, whether at school, in my community, in Japan, or in other countries. Now I had turned inward, concentrating only on myself and my work.

In the beginning I found it very difficult to make friends. For one thing, my roommates kept changing. I got along fine with my first roommate. Even though I could not express adequately how I felt, she seemed to understand me, because she was a minority student and was facing some of the same problems. When summer school ended, she was reassigned elsewhere; and for the fall I got a new roommate, who was Asian-American. We roomed together for the whole semester; but then she moved out to share quarters with another friend, and I was left without a roommate during the second semester. However, I found out that I got along with minority and other international students because they could relate to the problems I faced in being new and in a different culture. Gradually, I met most of these students, since there were very few on campus; and I began to spend more time with them.

It was harder to make friends with Americans. I noticed that I had to initiate conversations if there was to be any interaction between us. American students tend to stay away from people, like myself, who look and sound different from themselves. Not having any experience with other cultures, they cannot imagine the difficulties of living in another country. They don't understand the problems of having to become acclimated to different food, language, and customs. There is no way that they could know about the many regulations foreigners have to live under in the United States, such as work and financial aid restrictions.

The exceptions have been a few American students who are especially interested in Japan, who sought me out to talk about my country and its culture. Some of them were taking courses about Japan or studying the language and were planning to visit or had traveled to Japan. These friends, as well as the international students with whom I became close, were a great source of support for me and helped me open the door to outside.

With time, I became more accustomed to living on an American college campus. My English improved, and I gradually became more aware of what was going on around me. As I got acquainted with more people, especially with the international students, I started to spend less time in my room. With my new friends I attended campus activities, such as plays and special lectures; and I started to learn about various campus organizations.

By the fall semester of my second year, I joined an environmental awareness club and helped to organize a Japan-U.S. friendship club called Japonica, of which I am now president. I also started working in the library, where I had the opportunity to meet people with whom I have interests in common. By becoming more involved in campus life, I met more students and got to know more faculty and staff, as well as people from the larger community.

As a result of my increased awareness and participation, I have noticed that, while I am still basically a shy person, I have become somewhat more assertive and able to speak out on issues that are important to me. In classes I am now always ready to answer the professor's questions, and I feel less awkward when I am called on to say something in public. Conversations with my friends have become less formal, and I even have begun to enjoy chattering. I think that I have become more sociable.

Still, problems remain with which I struggle daily. Most have to do with a clash of values between my Japanese culture and mainstream American culture. For instance, my culture stresses harmony, cooperation, and negotiation, while in the United States there is more emphasis on interpersonal confrontation and argumentation. Thus, if I were to have a discussion in Japan about religion with people of differing views, we each might state what we believe in and then agree that each view has its merit, because religion is a private, individual matter.

In the United States, however, I have sat in on discussions where people tried to convince one another that their religion was the "right one" and attacked each other's point of view. In situations like this, I feel very frustrated and I usually keep my mouth shut. I would like to be able to say that I feel differently, that even though I may not agree with their beliefs, they can express them but not impose them on me. I don't feel that I can impose my views on anyone, and I wish

Americans would recognize this as well. When it comes to religion, especially, it seems that Americans are more serious, more absolute about their beliefs than are Japanese.

Another problem for me is that living in a different culture, I frequently cannot put into practice the basic moral principles I have been brought up with. For instance, one of these values is not to dwell on yourself but to focus on others and on the larger society. However, due to the pressures I am usually under as a student in this culture, it is very difficult to go beyond myself and my daily problems and to see the larger picture. Now that I take part in campus life, I am extremely busy with my studies, work in the library, and campus organizations. These demands lead me to neglect more important things, higher values such as understanding how I may be contributing to the community beyond myself and being aware that a larger world exists beyond the college campus.

It seems that the price I am paying for becoming too busy integrating myself into campus life is neglecting these important principles. I usually become aware that I have neglected my cultural values when things start going wrong, when I get over-extended or stressed out. For instance, I feel bad when a meeting doesn't get organized or I don't get an assignment in on time. I usually sit back and remind myself of my first priority and the special situation I am in: that my city sent me here and is supporting me, that my parents back home are thinking about me. I then go back to the starting point: why I came here, what I need to do, and what I want to do in the future. I try to broaden my view; and this gives me strength to go on, to organize my life better, and not to get bogged down in details.

One of the conflicts I have frequently experienced has to do with how Japanese and Americans view individual contributions to the common welfare. In Japan, you are not supposed to talk about the good deeds you have done, but rather the group or community should be able to recognize them if, indeed, you have made an important contribution. One is expected to be modest, humble, and not talk about oneself, except to admit one's inadequacies.

In the United States it is almost the reverse. You are encouraged to take pride in your accomplishments and to advertise them, to "sell yourself," rather than have the group acknowledge what you have done. In fact, the collective becomes aware of individual deeds because individuals talk about themselves. I have been told a number of times by Americans — students, faculty, and others — not to be so modest and to say more about what I am doing. Otherwise people will not know what I am contributing. However, having been brought up in Japan, if I am to talk about myself at all, I tend to downplay and trivialize my accomplishments by saying such things as "I didn't do anything at all," or "I didn't do it as well as I should have."

While I dislike the idea of having to call attention to myself, I must admit that after living in the United States for almost two years, I have mixed feelings about the notion of advertising one's own accomplishments. I feel now that if I do something good or worthwhile, it ought to be noticed. Sometimes people around me are just too busy to notice, however. So maybe I should be able to make them aware of my good deeds. I still wouldn't brag about myself, but I have come to realize that the Japanese emphasis on self-effacement may not be all that good, either. I think there could be a middle ground between the two cultural approaches.

In my daily life on campus, I still struggle sometimes with the notion of being true to what I want and believe in and having to make compromises in order to "fit in" with the general norms. For instance, I frequently have a great deal of class-related work, but I am likely to abandon it if a friend comes by and asks me to go along to a movie, lecture, or whatever. Even if I'd rather stay in my room and study, I am likely to go with the friend because it is expected of me. To get along well on campus, you need to socialize a great deal. Moreover, even if I may disagree fundamentally with something another student says, I usually don't verbalize my disagreement. I compromise and keep quiet. Even though this may not go directly against my beliefs, by keeping silent I realize that I could be providing tacit approval of ideas that I cannot accept.

I am a little concerned about how much this cross-cultural transition has affected me. I am willing to change, but I don't want to become like others just to be accepted. I am glad about some of the changes I see in myself. I no longer wait for others to come to me but am able to initiate conversations and ask for help. I can speak out more and express my opinions. And the longer I am here and the more I learn, I feel more and more comfortable, more "at home" in this culture. On the other hand, I have had to make some compromises in order to "fit in."

I see my attempts to adjust to a different culture as a kind of balancing act. On one end of the scale is my Japanese identity; on the other lies American culture and its lures. In order to preserve my integrity and not to assimilate, I keep myself somewhere between these two ends. I have changed, but I have not allowed myself to be swallowed up.

CARIBBEAN-AMERICAN TINDUCTION
TRANSITIONS

CHARMAINE BARNARD was born in Jamaica and came to live in New York City at the age of 11. After graduating from high school, she moved to a small, Midwestern town to go to college. She is a journalism major and sociology minor and hopes to make a career in broadcasting. She has a passion for music and dancing and has been active in college theater, campus publications, and electronic media. She expects to graduate in 1994.

I lived the early, formative years of my life in Jamaica under rather simple conditions. My family had no plumbing or modern appliances; and in order to get water, we had to walk for miles and carry it back home in pails. When it rained, we would put out a barrel to collect rain water to wash the dishes. I remember going to the market with my grandmother to sell vegetables, both of us carrying baskets on our heads.

The years I lived in Jamaica were some of the best of my life. Although at the time I took a lot for granted, I realize now the richness of my culture. For instance, the marketplace is one of the most interesting aspects of Jamaican culture, as everything of significance happens there. People buy and exchange food, clothing, and artifacts, as well as gossip and useful information. They meet friends and make important decisions there.

Life in Jamaica can be harsh. I remember one election time almost getting shot because the people who lived on my street were supporting rival candidates. They got into a heated argument and started shooting at one another. The house where I lived was located in the midst of this conflict. I was coming home from school, and a bullet ricocheted off a wall, narrowly missing me.

I grew up surrounded by positive female role models. The women in my family are very independent and strong. A favorite aunt of mine has five children, whom she is raising by herself. She holds two jobs in order to do this. My grandmother, who took care of me in Jamaica, is a feisty, vigorous woman who takes no nonsense from anyone.

Jamaican society is traditional. It is very family oriented, and children and youth are expected to respect and obey their elders. Children are disciplined from the time they learn to walk, and physical punishment is used readily. For instance, in school when children disobey the teacher, they get spanked and it hurts. I remember once coming home and telling my grandmother the teacher had given me a spanking; I got another one for having to be spanked in the first place.

You can imagine my culture shock when I came to New York and heard the way children spoke to their parents and other family members. I could not get over the attitude and the foul language they often used. It still bothers me when a younger person is disrespectful to someone older. I also could not accept the way students treated teachers. On my first day in a New York City school, one of the students went up to the teacher and said he did not want to do an assignment she had given to the class. When she insisted that he try to work on it, he cursed her out. I sat in amazement, not believing what I was hearing.

The transition from Jamaica to New York was not easy for me. Due to problems my mother was having, I moved in with relatives. This was not difficult in itself, because I was used to living in an extended family. Since early childhood there were always several adults − grandparents, aunts, and uncles − who helped raise me. What made it hard was that I left behind such a totally different way of life, a way of life that people in New York thought was primitive and inferior.

The neighborhood where I lived in New York was mostly African-American. I would sit on my steps, watching people argue and fight a lot; and I would wonder where neighborly love had gone. I missed the closely knit community I was a part of in Jamaica, where everyone knew each other and all the adults participated in raising all the children. Kids in Jamaica did not get away with much because there were too many people always watching over them.

When I first started school in New York, the kids all wanted to know where I was from; and I told them proudly that I was Jamaican. They began to make comments that Jamaica was a tiny island somewhere in the ocean and that people there ran around with no clothes on. From then on, I did not disclose readily where I came from. School in New York was difficult at first because the children would pick on me, and I found myself fighting a lot to maintain my dignity.

Ironically, a few years later, when I was in high school, everybody wanted to be Jamaican. Jamaican music, dancing, and food became very fashionable among African-Americans in New York. Now the kids were interested in my background. It made me think how shallow and phony some people in this culture can be. First, they didn't care for me when they thought my culture was somehow inferior to theirs; and then when Jamaican culture became popular, I became sought after. This has taught me to be very cautious when it comes to making friends.

When I started high school, students had to be escorted to the trains by police officers due to frequent incidents of gang violence. The walls of my school were painted with blood. Some students were shot and some teachers were badly beaten. New York can be a very violent place to live. I had to keep my eye on people and be careful wherever I went. The advantage of living in a place like New York, however, is that it has many diverse cultures. I loved seeing people from all over the world, going to ethnic festivals, hearing so many languages being spoken, listening to music from different countries, and trying different foods.

The second cross-cultural transition I made was from New York to a small, Midwestern college campus. I did not apply to any college until April of my senior year in high school, because it did not even occur to me that it was an option I could pursue. No one in my family had been to college, and most of my friends could not afford to go. However, I had an academic advisor who had graduated from a small college in the Midwest; and he advised me to apply there, as well as to several other places. He insisted that my grades were good enough and that I should have no problem being accepted. I was reluctant to apply to colleges in the Midwest, but he encouraged me to visit the school he graduated from, because it had a strong journalism program and I was interested in broadcasting.

During my brief visit to the campus, I realized that it would not be easy for me to spend four years of my life at this small college. The campus is isolated, there is no public transportation, and I would not be able to afford a car. Being black, I would be one of a handful of minority students in an almost all-white institution. The town surrounding the college also is almost all white. Despite these serious obstacles, I was attracted to the college because it seemed so green, calm, and peaceful, a stark contrast to New York City. Perhaps I was reminded somewhat of my former life in Jamaica. Moreover, the college offered me a good financial package; and so I decided to come.

At first everyone seemed really friendly. Students I didn't even know would smile and say, "Hello, how are you?" to me as I walked across the campus mall between classes. But I soon discovered that the friendliness was superficial. After the initial greetings, there was no attempt to get to know me better. I tried to initiate some interactions, but people did not seem interested. Consequently, my first semester was extremely lonely. I attended classes, and the rest of the time I spent in my room. I even took up a hobby: pillow-making. I must have made about a hundred pillows in the course of that semester just to fill time.

I felt very isolated that first semester. Apart from occasional casual conversations with other students, there was no one I could talk to seriously about what was going on in my life, no one I could call a friend. After a while I started to feel unappreciated and unattractive. No one really looked at me, no one said anything of significance to me, no one complimented me. When I went home for Christmas that year, I stepped off the plane at JFK airport and some guy said, "Hey, baby, you look good." It was like I became alive again. Someone found me attractive after all.

During that Christmas vacation, I got enough affirmation that I was a "regular" person; so when I returned to the college in January, I decided that I was not going to let the students' aloofness bother me. I concentrated on my studies and got a job at the bookstore to fill in time in the evenings. And after a while, I found that I could just bury my emotions and not feel anything anymore. A person my age should feel attracted to other people, should have fun, should enjoy college life. But I was able to cut all that off and not feel a thing. An emotional blank — that's what I was that year.

Then I returned to New York again for the summer and was able to release my emotions. Among my friends, among people of my own race, I felt comfortable and accepted. I contemplated switching colleges and maybe going somewhere bigger where I would not be a member of such a small minority. But friends of mine who had gone to large universities were having problems, too, and were looking for other schools. I was doing well academically if not socially. They, on the other hand, were getting low grades as well as encountering racism. I figured then that I would get all my affection for the year in the summer and go back to school fortified, ready to face the loneliness once again.

106

I returned to the college in the fall with a new resolve: I would focus my energies on academics. But I would also try to get involved in various activities on campus. I love to sing and dance, and so I tried out for a part in a musical play. I got the part; and through participation in long rehearsals, I not only filled in time but got to know some of the other players. I started getting invited to parties, and many people became genuinely friendly to me.

I also joined a campus organization for the support of minorities. Through this group I got to know most of the other minority students who attended the college and discovered that I was not alone in what I had experienced. Like me, most of them felt isolated and lonely. Even those who were better integrated into campus life still felt like outsiders. We were able to form a little support group for each other. I discovered that there was another black woman of Jamaican origin on campus, and we became good friends.

Participation in campus activities was a vehicle for getting involved in the co-curricular aspects of college existence and for making friends. It also opened up a different view of college life in the Midwest for which I was scarcely prepared. For instance, when I was first invited to campus parties, I assumed that there would be lots of dancing and just plain innocent fun. The parties I attended in New York were essentially dancing parties. We would all dance together in a group and teach each other new steps. Sometimes there would be alcohol around, but no one would abuse it.

At my college, however, parties focus on drinking and getting drunk. There are beer and drinking games. What I found really alien is that getting drunk seemed to be the entire reason for campus parties. Having fun equaled drinking heavily.

Both Jamaica and the New York community I came from are cultures where alcohol is not prohibited — in fact, it is used rather freely — but children and youth do not abuse it. In the Midwest, and I understand in many other parts of the United States, drinking is a favorite pastime for college students. I think that could be because alcohol is so restricted when American kids are still at home. When they go to college, drinking becomes a sign of rebellion and growing up. In any case, alcohol abuse occurs frequently at my college; and I have had a difficult time dealing with it. I try to avoid drinking parties as much as possible.

Another difficulty I encountered after getting out more and participating in campus life has been in establishing intimate relationships with men. For a black woman on a predominantly white campus, relationships are hard to come by, since there are so few black men. I am a bit apprehensive about dating someone of another race. A friend of mine had a very bad experience when she was going with a white boyfriend. It turned out that he was dating her because he wanted to find out what it was like to be with a black woman, and he was also rebelling against his parents, who did not approve of interracial relationships. As soon as he got tired of her, he told her of his motives for dating her and dumped her. She was devastated.

I have tried dating white men but never felt comfortable, not being sure of their intentions. I could not tell whether they wanted to go out with me because they liked me for myself or because they were curious to see what it would be like to date a black woman or to have sex with her. Consequently, my college dating experiences have been very limited. In my sophomore year, I met an African-American student whom I liked very much; and we dated for several months. I was fortunate to have this relationship.

As I got to know more students better, I found that I frequently had to deal with questions about racial and cultural differences. People were curious about such things as how I perm my hair, what certain words really mean in the black vernacular, what foods African-Americans and Jamaicans eat, and the like. At first I felt annoyed and was sometimes incredulous at the questions, but I soon realized that it was good for them to ask me. Rather than wondering why or thinking that people of another race were doing things the wrong way, by questioning me directly these students were able to learn about my culture. In the process I became friends with some of them. I came to appreciate their honesty and candor. Over time, several female students who seemed most curious to know things about me became part of a kind of support group, composed of people who could understand what I was experiencing, and helped me to work through things.

Still another sensitive area for me to deal with on a predominantly white campus has been classroom interaction when there is a minority student present. It seems that even one black student in class can be a kind of inhibiting factor in discussions. For instance, in an economics class the professor was trying to illustrate the basis on which landlords might decide to accept or reject potential renters. He asked a white male student whether he would prefer to rent a house to a rich or a poor family, a family with or without children, a black or a white family. The student answered the first two parts of the question, but then turned around to look at the only black person in the room and would not answer the part about race.

I have been in several classroom situations where race was being discussed and both the professor and the students were visibly uncomfortable because of my presence. I had the feeling that the conversation would have taken a very different turn had I not been there. There have been instances where I or another minority student is asked by the professor to comment on an issue from "the African-American perspective." I find this ludicrous. It is like asking a white student to provide a "white point of view" on something, which no one would do because everyone recognizes that the group "whites" is extremely diverse. African-Americans are also very heterogeneous, but few white people here seem to realize this.

Being part of such a small minority on a practically all-white campus has made me much more aware of being black. It is not that my race had not been a part of my identity before I came to the college, but since I arrived it has become a dominant factor. It seems to be always right there: You are black and everything you do and say, how other people perceive you, is mediated through your race. While I am proud of who I am, including belonging to my race, I often wish that people would just relate to me as a human being who is both like them as well as different, and not pay attention to the color of my skin.

While making this transition from New York to the Midwest has not been easy, I also recognize that I have benefited in the process. I am receiving a solid education in an institution of higher learning that provides a great deal of personal attention and care. I have learned a tremendous amount about how people in the Midwest live and what their values and priorities are. I have come to have no use for stereotypes. I have come to appreciate other cultures and have no prejudice against any group.

With each of the cultural changes I have made, first from Jamaica to New York and then from New York to the Midwest, I gradually felt my mind opening to embrace more of the world and the different people in it. I have come to understand that we are all human beings, essentially the same at the core, but different because of our cultures and personalities. I have come to respect both the similarities and the differences.

If I had to do it all over again, I would still choose to come to my college in the Midwest. However, if I could change anything, I would wish for an easier transition upon arrival on campus. To help make the change less traumatic for minority students, a college could provide a support system made up of other minority students, as well as those in the majority who want to be involved. A program needs to be in place through which new minority students would be helped by old-timers to get involved in campus life.

I also think that more knowledge about African-Americans and other American minorities needs to be integrated into the curriculum. I would feel less alien on campus if more courses dealt with black culture and history. Minority students in general would welcome such programs as African-American, Hispanic, Asian-American, and Native Studies. Emphasis on intercultural and international studies sends a message that all cultures are valued. Those of us who are in the minority could find affirmation for where we come from and who we are through such programs.

I know that I am not alone in what I have experienced. College administrators and others who are concerned about how to ease cultural transitions for students should talk to people like myself and others about what would make such transitions easier. There is no need for students to go through extreme loneliness, emotional withdrawal, and pain when they find themselves in a new cultural environment. I was lucky. I managed to get through the initial tough stage in the process. Many others gave up and went home, only to live with bitter memories and unresolved conflicts. With a little forethought and determination, it is possible to make cross-cultural transitions for minority students more positive and successful.

BLACK AND WHITE

SHIRLEY ANN WILLIAMS, JR., is African-American and a native of Queens, New York. She traveled extensively throughout the United States with her family in her childhood and teens. After graduating from high school in New York, she entered a predominantly white college in a small town in the Midwest, from which she expects to graduate with a major in broadcast journalism and a minor in sociology. She hopes to make a career in social work.

I lived the first 18 years of my life in a culturally diverse environment. In my neighborhood there were blacks, Hispanics, Chinese, Poles, Germans, and several other groups. The primary and secondary schools I attended were racially mixed, and I had the opportunity to get to know people my age who grew up in very different home cultures. Although I consider myself to be African-American, I actually have a multicultural heritage: my mother is half-Irish and my paternal grandmother is Cherokee Indian. My parents, my three sisters, and I also traveled a lot. We would always go somewhere interesting and unique for vacations, sometimes spending one or two weeks in a small town or visiting a large city. Being exposed to different people and new places taught me to be tolerant of differences and to treat people without prejudice.

When I was in my senior year in high school and considering where I might go to college, I met an alumnus of my school who was enrolled at a college in the Midwest. He came back to recruit students and described the merits of his college in glowing terms. I was intrigued. I applied to the school and was asked to come for an interview. Amazingly, the college was able to fly me and my mother out for a weekend. We both were very impressed by what we saw and heard. While I noticed immediately that almost everyone at the college was white, the facilities and curriculum appeared to be excellent, and everyone was extremely friendly and helpful. The college also was able to provide me with scholarships and financial aid. I decided to come and looked forward to the fall when I would embark on my great educational adventure.

When I first arrived at the college, the staff, faculty, and students seemed friendly enough; but several incidents occurred during the first year that made me doubt whether I had made the right choice of colleges. Soon after I got to campus, I met a young woman my age who told me that she had never seen a black person before, except on television. She grew up in an all-white town and went to all-white schools until she came to college and found that there was a handful of blacks. She wanted to touch my hair and skin and asked all sorts of personal questions. I was not sure how to react to this. I had never experienced anything like it before. She made me feel very uncomfortable; and yet, in a strange way, I could appreciate her curiosity. After realizing what a sheltered life this person had led, I was no longer upset, but rather amused.

An incident with a roommate was not so amusing, however. I shared a dorm room with a white female student. One day, the resident assistant came to me to say that my roommate had complained about not being able to get along with me because I had too many posters on the wall. I found this very peculiar, to say the least. I could not understand how the number of posters I had put up could have anything to do with how the two of us were getting along. I had made sure that all my posters were on the wall next to my bed and none of her space was being invaded. When I confronted her with the complaint, she said that she just did not like all the posters. When I pressed why, she finally admitted that she did not like them because they were all of black people and she just could not deal with having so many black faces stare at her from the wall.

I lost my cool and told her she was racist. She replied that she certainly was not and that, furthermore, she did not want me to touch her stuff. I never had touched any of her things, so this was a final blow. I told her she would have to move. She was a sophomore and I was only a first-year student, so she tried to pull rank and have me move out. But I stuck to my resolve, and in the end she took her stuff and left.

Another discouraging encounter took place between me and a professor with whom I was taking a class in the journalism department. In response to something I wrote, he told me that I would never be a writer and would not be able to finish the major. He advised me to switch to another major. At first I was shocked and hurt. Then I remembered that my father was also told by several people that he could not write, and then he ended up writing a book that was published. I became more determined to stick with my studies and to do what I had to in order to get through. I vowed that someday I, too, would have a book and that I would come back and show it to this professor.

Still another disappointing thing I noticed during the first year was that even though many people appeared to be friendly, they would gossip about me behind my back. For no reason I could see, they would say that I was stuck up or dumb or mean. I happened to overhear a couple of conversations where I was mentioned in this manner; and later, when I made friends, my friends would tell me how others talked about me. I felt very hurt by this because I had not given any reason to these people to say negative things about me. They talked about me without knowing me at all.

In the environment I grew up in, if somebody didn't like you, they would tell you that and let you know why. They wouldn't pretend to be one thing to your face and another behind your back. People were more direct with one another in New York. So I came to the conclusion that there is a lot of superficial friendliness and phoniness in the Midwest. I don't like to generalize like this, but my experience has led me to this opinion.

I also encountered some awkward classroom situations. Since there were very few minority students on campus, I often would be the only black person in a class. During discussions, professors would sometimes turn to me to ask how blacks would feel about an issue. The first time it happened, I was so shocked that I could not answer at all. The second time, I said that I could speak only for myself and not for all persons of my race. I suppose that white professors sometimes assume that all black people speak with one voice and have the same experience. I think they would understand how I felt if someone asked them to be spokespersons for the entire white race. I found, too, that my presence in the classroom sometimes inhibited discussions. White students would avoid expressing their opinions on such issues as interracial dating, welfare recipients, and poverty when I was in class. I was aware of this, since I heard enough outside of class to know that they really had strong feelings on these subjects.

Being a black female on a predominantly white campus has had its special problems. There are very few black males, and you're out of luck if you don't happen to like any of them. Interracial dating does occur; but it is very stressful, because it's highly visible and there is a general attitude among the students against it. My solution has been to have a boyfriend back home in New York.

By the end of the first year, I was thinking seriously about changing colleges. I considered transferring to a black college. I even made some initial inquiries but discovered that I would lose an important number of credits if I moved to another institution. When I returned to New York over the summer, I carefully weighed the pros and cons of staying at the college. It seemed that the balance was on the negative side; but then, when I started to consider what I gained from my experience, I suddenly became aware of the positives. I realized that when I got out of college, the majority of employers were going to be white; and if I could learn to function reasonably well in a mostly white college, I would have a better chance of surviving in the "real world" of predominantly white institutions.

I also knew that the quality of education I was receiving was very good; and if I made it through the four years, I would be well-prepared to enter my field upon graduation. Toward the end of the year, I became involved in a student organization for the support of minorities. Through this group I found people who were sympathetic and truly friendly. I also acquired a kind of mentor through a program that tries to pair students with people from the faculty, staff, and members of the larger community. So I had a beginning support system. I decided to stay and tough it out.

The longer I have been at the college (I am now a senior), the easier it has become for me to deal with prejudice and racism. I realized that most people are prejudiced inadvertently, not because they want to hurt me and others of my race, but because they don't know any better. They were raised in practically all-white towns or neighborhoods and had no experience of racial and cultural diversity. I think these white students would benefit greatly from spending a few months in New York City or Chicago or Los Angeles. I almost think it ought to be mandatory for all students to spend some time living in other cultures, learning how other people live, and learning to appreciate others' differences. This would go a long way toward changing their attitudes.

Meanwhile, I have tried to rise above the prejudice that has been directed at me and to treat people individually, rather than turning around and treating them the way they have treated me. I have discovered that once I am able to break through the barriers of race and culture by insisting that I am a human being in my own right and that I should be treated as such, some people rise to the occasion. As a result, I have been able to form true friendships with people of other races and to feel a greater sense of personal dignity and worth.

I realize that my presence on campus may have had some impact on the students with whom I've come in contact. Inside and outside the classroom, I have had the opportunity to talk about my experiences and to express my opinions. Usually, they are very different from those of the majority of students. For instance, in a discussion of Spike Lee's movie, *Do the Right Thing*, I told my classmates about some incidents of racial tension I had seen in New York. I think this made the situation in the movie more believable to them, and they realized they had been living very sheltered lives.

On the other hand, I have changed, too, as a result of living in a different cultural environment. For one thing, I have become somewhat more laid back. Back home, people tend to be more frantic because they live in a big, teeming, sometimes overwhelming city. Here in the Midwest, people don't hurry as much. Yes, they are busy. But they take the time to notice what's going on around them. I also have picked up the habit of greeting people I don't know. When I go home, I unconsciously say "hello" to strangers on the street. People back East have said to me that I must not be from around there since I do this, and I have gotten suspicious stares from strangers.

If I had to do it over again, I think I would choose to go to a black college or at least to one that had an extensive black studies program. In a predominantly white school, the pressures are enormous to fit into the white, mainstream culture. Even though I have resisted, I have not had the support of a black community that could uphold my culture on an equal footing. While the college has offered occasional courses dealing with black literature, I would have benefited from taking part in a black studies program through which I could learn more about my heritage. That might have offered me a base and a ready-made support system. I believe that programs like this are very important for largely white colleges to attract and keep larger numbers of minority students. Without this support, life for a minority student on a mostly white campus is a never-ending struggle that grinds us down, a struggle that only a few can survive.

I always give credit to my own upbringing for having come this far, for having survived this difficult transition. Because I have been around so many different types of people and because of the way my parents raised me, I try not to prejudge others. And I expect them to treat me the way I treat them — without reference to skin color or ethnic group. My expectations are not always met; and when they are not, I deal with the situation as best I can.

PART III

Reflections of a Cultural Commuter

Birgit Brock-Utne provided the keynote address for the Women and Cross-Cultural Transitions Conference, from which the preceding narratives were drawn. In this concluding chapter, Professor Brock-Utne has adapted her address to include her reflections on the women's narratives.

Birgit Brock-Utne was born in Norway but has lived for extended periods of time in the United States, Tanzania, and Germany. She is a social scientist and activist, who is currently an associate professor at the Institute for Educational Research at the University of Oslo in Norway. She recently completed a five-year appointment at the University of Dar es Salaam in Tanzania and a one-term visit at Antioch University in Ohio.

She has studied in the United States at Stanford University in California and at the University of Illinois, where she received her master's degree in education. She also has a doctorate from Oslo University. She has written numerous articles and several books, the most recent being *Feminist Perspectives on Peace and Peace Education* (Pergamon, 1989). In addition, she has served the international community as a consultant to UNESCO, OECD, the European Council, the Nordic Council, and the United Nations.

REFLECTIONS OF A CULTURAL COMMUTER
by Birgit Brock-Utne

The diverse accounts of women's cross-cultural transitions in this volume are wonderful and moving. They demonstrate the enriching experiences connected to lives lived in two or more cultures. Complex dimensions and new outlooks are revealed. But they also demonstrate how the longing for the home country, for the language of the first lullabies, never leaves a person who has made what, by all indications, seems to be a successful cross-cultural transition.

Traveling on a train from Seattle to San Francisco many years ago, I happened to sit next to an old woman. When she started speaking to me, I noticed that her intonation and pronunciation were so Norwegian that I decided she had to be Norwegian. So in my next sentence to her I spoke in Norwegian. She looked at me with tears in her eyes and said in her broken English and with the same Norwegian intonation: "Yes, I am Norwegian; but I came to this country 50 years ago and have hardly spoken Norwegian since. I understand everything you say, and please go on talking Norwegian to me; but I am not able to speak Norwegian anymore. It is sad because I don't speak English well either, and I never really felt at home here." I pitied her and imagined the agony of one who is culturally homeless.

Compared to her, I feel lucky, since no one hearing me speak Norwegian would doubt that I am Norwegian. Yet my own background is culturally mixed; and I have, for the last five to six years, been traveling back and forth constantly between four cultures and four languages. My reflections on the topic of cross-cultural transitions are based on my recent life as a cultural commuter.

During the 24 hours before coming to the Women and Cross-Cultural Transitions Conference, I was in contact with all of the four cultures that are so much a part of me. My husband drove me to the airport in Dar es Salaam, Tanzania, in the morning; and we naturally spoke Norwegian as we rode. We talked about Norway, about moving back to our country after 5½ years in Africa. On the plane I met a Tanzanian colleague and became immersed in the problems of the University of Dar es Salaam. I spoke Kiswahili all the way from Dar es Salaam to Frankfurt am Main, Germany, the town where my mother grew up and also where I have studied.

In Frankfurt, I had a layover at the airport hotel and enjoyed a relaxed dinner with a German peace researcher and friend who is much like a brother to me. We spoke in German, which, as it is the language of my mother, is close to my heart. We are about the same age, and our experiences of the Second World War and the years directly thereafter affected us while we were at tender ages and have formed us both.

And then I came to the United States, where I first studied for a year as a teenager in California and then took my master's at the University of Illinois, where I lived with my husband and eldest son. Since then, I have been back lecturing at various colleges and universities including, most recently, a visit as Professor of Peace Studies at Antioch College.

The four countries between which I have been commuting are Norway, Germany, Tanzania, and the United States. The cultures and languages are Norwegian, German, Kiswahili, and American English. Three of the countries belong to the affluent Western industrialized world; but one of them, Germany, has a history of aggressive wars in this century, including military occupation of the country I grew up in, Norway. The fourth country, Tanzania, is one of the poorest countries in the world as measured by traditional economic indicators.

What have I gained from commuting between and among these four cultures? What have I learned? And what problems have I encountered?

The Status of the Cultures Involved in the Cross-Cultural Transitions

A theme that appears in several of the preceding accounts has to do with the status of the cultures involved in the cross-cultural transitions. It is easier to be an American of Norwegian descent than it is to be one of Hispanic or African descent. It is regarded as charming in Norway to hear somebody speak Norwegian with a French accent. But when someone speaks Norwegian with a Pakistani accent, the speaker is likely to be ridiculed.

I have benefited from the positive stereotypes of Norwegians in the United States, Germany, and Tanzania. But being half-German, I also have experienced what it feels like to be ashamed of one's culture.

I remember my favorite German lullabies, the ones my mother sang to me while I was a young child; but I also remember that I was taught that I must never speak German in the street. I remember when we started to study German in school that my classmates were told by their parents to get the worst possible grades in that subject. I got good grades in German, and I loved the language.

My mother speaks Norwegian with a German accent; and I remember hearing somebody ask her, "Where is that accent from?" I also clearly remember her answer, "You may guess and just come up with the meanest guess you can think of."

In my childhood years I learned that being of German descent was more to be ashamed of than proud of. I also learned that there were fine Germans. I grew to love my German grandmother, whom I did not see for many years. I learned to appreciate the language, the rhymes, the lullabies, and the poetry. I came to love Goethe and to learn the poetry of Heinrich Heine by heart. I came to appreciate the tenderness I found in German friends, the politeness, the humor, the good manners coupled with punctuality and hard work.

Whether one can be proud or ashamed of the culture one comes from may determine whether one is more likely to integrate into the new culture. Not wanting to identify with her or his culture of origin may motivate a cross-cultural traveler to take on the customs and values of the new society. I have noticed, for instance, that Germans who are ashamed of the war history of Germany prefer to carry European passports. Danes, who are more proud of their country, dislike having to carry European passports, preferring Danish passports. On the other hand, there are those who cross over into a new culture from a country or subculture considered low in status who want to hold onto their cultural heritage but find pressures against it.

As several accounts in this collection indicate, it is indeed a difficult dilemma when the cross-cultural traveler does not want to assimilate but finds contempt in the host culture for the customs and values of his or her culture of origin. (See, for example, Charmaine Barnard's account of her transition from Jamaica to New York.)

What One Learns About One's Own Culture
When One Becomes Part of a New Culture

Customs. When I was 19 years old, I was awarded a one-year scholarship to Stanford University in California. I lived in a sorority and made life-long friends. One early experience from my Stanford years became for me an important eye-opener.

I came from a home with a rather strict adherence to conventional and continental European table manners. I had been brought up to know that it is extremely rude to keep elbows on the table and that the knife and the fork should be used throughout the meal and then placed side by side on the plate when one finished eating. I was brought up to know that to first cut the food then lay the knife aside and make use of only the fork during the rest of the meal was regarded as bad table manners, impolite, and disagreeable.

Very much to my surprise, I noticed that the other girls in the sorority I lived in at Stanford all had those "bad" table manners, even though most came from very well-to-do homes. Watching them eat almost made me lose my appetite. I was surprised that they had not learned better table manners at home. Maybe their parents had not had time to teach them proper manners? I wondered if perhaps Americans did not care about eating correctly. I continued to eat the way I was taught at home and thought that after some time, when they watched me eat in this cultivated manner every day, they would see how much nicer it looked and would begin to imitate me.

It came as a shock to me when the president of our house one day after dinner took me aside and said that she had to tell me something in private. "This might be embarrassing for you, and I am so sorry I have to tell you," she said, "but several of the girls in the house have asked me to teach you correct table manners. They lose their appetite watching you eat. I shall now show you how you do it." And she demonstrated: "First you cut up the food with the knife. Then you place the knife at the side and continue with the fork in the right hand. Your left hand should be placed in your lap."

I was dumbfounded. She was teaching me to eat the way that my parents had told me was rude and unseemly. But the experience — at such an early age — was important for me. It increased my tolerance for different ways of doing things. It decreased my adherence to the perception that there were right ways and wrong ways.

When I later learned that most people in the world do not eat with forks and knives at all — that many eat with chop sticks, but most eat with just their hands — it did not come so much as a shock for me. I first learned to eat with just my hands in India and discovered that there were certain rules for doing that, too. One should use only the right hand and only the tips of the fingers. To get food into one's palm was impolite.

Last year I was a keynote lecturer at a seminar in Tanzania. After my talk, we all went to have lunch. There were six tables with plates for all the participants. Only one of the tables had forks and knives. I was asked to be seated at that table together with some high officials of the Ministry of Education. They laughed and felt relieved when I decided not to use the fork and knife but to eat in the African manner, using just my hands. Our hands were washed before we had the meal and again afterward, according to custom.

Values. One learns through living in different cultures that customs, manners, and tastes differ. One also learns that values differ. I find that the greatest benefit I have had from my life as a cultural commuter, especially from my life in Tanzania, is the heightened awareness of the fact that there may be good reasons to question values inherent in the Western way of living. This theme is explored also by several of the international students in Part II of this volume.

One day, when I was sitting in the tea garden drinking tea and eating *mandazi* (a type of doughnut) with my students at the University of Dar es Salaam, one of them suddenly looked at me and said:

"You know, Professor, I've heard that in your country and other industrialized and developed countries, when people get really old, they are stowed away in a house where there are only old people. Sometimes that house may be far away from where they used to live. They are left alone in that house to die. They are seldom visited by anyone. *Ni kweli?* Is it true?"

I noticed that the whole tea garden was eagerly awaiting my answer. The way the question was formulated, people living in the West seemed like monsters, discarding their elderly parents. It was difficult to defend this system. I was aware of how bad it sounded when I said that there was usually no one left in the family to take care of the elderly parents, that nobody had time for them.

"No time for your parents? How can you say such a thing? They gave you their time when you were young and helpless. They were awake with you if you had pains in the night. They fed you when you were hungry. They saw to it that you had clothes, that you got to school. Don't you feel it is now your turn to repay them? When you say you don't have time, is that because of the so-called 'development'? Maybe we should think twice about becoming developed."

The question, my attempt to explain our system of homes for the elderly, and the arguments from my students made me think. They made me wonder about the type of society we have created in the West. The way my Tanzanian colleagues and friends handled death and lived out their grief taught me much and had me question the way we in the Western world handle these phenomena.

When my elderly father died back in Norway, I informed my dean at the university and left for Norway with my husband the same night in order to spend a couple of days with my mother and then to participate in the funeral. The day after I left, my colleagues from the faculty of education came to my home in Dar es Salaam in a big van. They knew that I had gone to Norway, but they told my stepdaughter they wanted to show their respect to "a house in grief."

Some days after I came back to the university, a messenger came to me in the tea room with a thick envelope full of Tanzanian money, 100- and 200-shilling notes, and a letter from all my colleagues showing how much each had contributed. The envelope contained almost 8,000 Tanzanian shillings (about 25 U.S. dollars). I felt embarrassed, since the amount was a very large sum of money to my colleagues, the equivalent of a month's salary for a professor on the faculty. (My own monthly salary was 70 times as much, since I got my normal university salary from home in Norwegian currency.)

At first I did not know how to react, but one of my good friends on the staff said, "You must under no circumstances give the money back to us. We have collected money to show that you are one of us. This is what we do to help each other if there is a death in the family. Death costs money. You have to feed the people who come and stay with you."

I was touched. I could not use the money the way it was intended, since the funeral had already been held in my mother's home. But I bought a beautiful Makonde carving — a "mama Tanzania" — and gave it to my mother from my colleagues.

When a colleague died, other colleagues went to stay with his widow until after the funeral; and we all went to the hospital to accompany his body to the funeral. In the church we took turns passing the open coffin. There we stood for a minute or two and looked at him, saying good-bye while hymns were sung.

I celebrated feasts to the honor of the dead a month after my colleague had died, and a year afterward. There were parties with lots of good food and singing. In Madagascar I was told how the dead would be dug up from the graves for special occasions, for example, when a new baby was born into the family or there was a particular anniversary. The bodies would be swathed in a cloth that preserved them for a long time. They would be reburied and dug up again as long as there were people living who had known them. The missionaries I spoke with condemned this practice and stamped it "heathen." But somehow it made sense to me.

In Kiswahili there are two words for a dead person, a *mzimu* or a *mfu*. A *mzimu* is a person who is physically dead but is quite alive in the memories of living persons. *Mzimu* really means "one in good health." You often ask a person you meet in a Kiswahili culture, "Mzima?" Are you in good health? And the person will answer back, "Mzima." Yes, I am in good health. A *mzimu* (plural *wazimu*) is a spirit who is in good health, a spirit who is living within you and of whom you have memory pictures. In English, one translation could be "a living-dead."

When there is no one left in the world who has a memory-picture of a dead person, that person is no longer a *mzimu* but a *mfu* (plural *wafu*), a truly dead person. The dead people who are celebrated in Tanzania, who influence the lives of the living, who are consulted, are the *wazimu*, not the *wafu*.

I learned in Tanzania the importance of letting the dead continue to play an important part in the lives of the living. It is easier to cope with grief if a dear, deceased person continues to provide the occasion for family gatherings and is kept alive by those who knew her or him. My family and I recently held a gathering in remembrance of my oldest son's 31st birthday. He was killed in a car accident 10 years ago but is still a very important person in all our lives.

For Tanzanians, the *wazimu* are not only alive in memories but can take an active role in the lives of their relatives and friends. Sitting in the tea garden one day, one of my graduate students at the University of Dar es Salaam told me the following story:

> When my grandfather felt that he was about to die, he asked me to come to his hut. I was just 17 at that time. There were many family members gathered in his hut. He said to me, "I want you to promise me that when you marry and get sons, you will name them after me." I promised to do that.
>
> He died some months later. It took almost 10 years before I married. The year after I married, my son was born and I named him after my grandfather, as I had promised. I then had a daughter. The third child was again a son. I thought that I had satisfied my grandfather's wish when it came to the first son, so now we could take a name from my wife's side for the

second son. So we did, even though some of the older people in my family reminded me that grandfather had said I should name my sons after him. And he had several first names. I could have used one of them. I defended myself and said I felt I had obeyed his wish having named my first son after him.

But, you know, the day after that child was named he started developing all sort of illnesses. He got malaria twice and we thought he would die. If there was a cold around, he would get it. We went to doctors who gave him medicine. He would recover, but soon he would get sick again. We then took him to a *mganga* (shaman) who said it was clear that the reason that the boy was sick so much was that his father had not obeyed the wish of the grandfather to name his sons after him.

"If you want your son to be in good health, you have to give a big party and rename the boy, taking one of the other names of your grandfather," said the mganga.

So I did. Since then the boy has been in good health all the time.

"How would you explain that?" the student asked me. He was convinced that it was the *mzimu* of the grandfather that was asserting itself.

I discovered that all of my students shared his belief. They did not believe, as I do, that the *wazimu* are only playing a part in the lives of the living because we allow them to, but that they do in fact still exist around us and intervene in our lives, helping us or correcting us as they deem appropriate.

Greetings. A basic thing one usually learns when traveling between cultures is the appropriate ways of greeting people. I believe that the greetings in a culture are a gateway to an understanding of that culture.

In the Kiswahili culture of Tanzania, there is a special expression of respect used by younger people when greeting those who are older. The younger person says, "Shikamo," which means, "I would like to wash your feet"; whereupon the older person says, "Marahaba," which means, "Do it seven times."

Greetings in Tanzania take a long time. You are expected to inquire about the family, life, work, and health of the person. If you have not seen the person for some days, you ask how he or she has been since you last visited. The Western way of coming quickly to the point or rather directly making a request is regarded as impolite. One has to create the right atmosphere first, get to know the mood of the other person before one can come forward with a request or a question. This smooth way of starting a conversation often seems like a waste of time to the impatient Westerner. But not paying respect to such an aspect of the Kiswahili culture often will prevent one from achieving his or her aim. One will be regarded as abrupt and imposing.

Having to go through a lot of greetings and small talk before coming forward with your appeal used to be the correct behavior also in the Norwegian countryside when I was young. I remember that my mother, who came from a large city in Germany, had great difficulty adapting to this custom. If she wanted to have one of the local women sew something for her, my mother would just go to her and make the request, whereupon she got a negative answer. So she learned the hard way that if she wanted a positive answer, she had to inquire about the woman's health, about her children, about her husband who was on a ship, about the neighbors, and about the cherry-picking. It could be a conversation that took several hours. Finally, when she had already put on her coat and was about to go, she would say quite casually, "And, by the way, you would probably not have the time to sew a blouse for Birgit?" The woman would answer just as casually, "I think it will be hard, but I shall see." And my mother then knew that an agreement had been reached.

The similarities between my mother's experience in the Norwegian countryside almost 50 years ago and the ones I had in Tanzania are striking and make me reflect. Through the so-called "development" toward higher productivity and greater efficiency, we seem to be losing ways of communicating that probably led to less tension and interpersonal conflict than do those methods we tend to use today.

Having been brought up by my German mother to observe punctuality, always being on time and planning ahead, it was not easy for me to get used to my African friends, who would come half an hour and sometimes an hour or two late to a party to which they had been invited. I had to learn that there was something called "African time." That would include coming late for appointments.

This lack of strict punctuality, however, was déjà vu for me. I had become familiar with the phenomenon when I lived in the Norwegian north for seven years. People in the capital of Oslo in the south, where I came from, would talk about "North-Norwegian time," implying that people in the north had a lackadaisical attitude toward punctuality.

Once I had invited a good Tanzanian friend to a dinner party at my house. People had been invited for 7 p.m., and I told him that we would first start with cocktails and then have dinner. Knowing that he normally was late, I said it did not matter if he came at seven.

But he had to be there before 8:30, I insisted, because that was when I was going to give a speech in Kiswahili and I wanted him to listen to it. But he did not come. I waited and waited for him. Around 9:30, I felt I could not wait any longer and gave the speech. He came around 10:00 while we were having dessert. He was smiling as always. I was upset and, without the usual greeting, said, "Umechelewa." You have come too late. He smiled, pointed to the food that was still there, and said, "Hata. Chakula kipo." No, not at all — there is still food left. According to him, as long as there was still food, he could not have come too late.

The same friend questioned my upbringing when it came to my constant planning ahead — in a year I would do this; on my next sabbatical in three years I would do that. "You white people with your constant planning," he would say. "You have almost planned your whole life. Does that not feel like being dead? What more is there to live for? The excitement of life is just that things happen. Maybe the world does not even exist. The past exists; the present exists. Enjoy the past, enjoy the present, and do not worry or plan the future."

Often I think he is right. My many talks with him have led me to question my own planning and not to plan so much for the long term.

"As a Woman My Country Is the World"

In her wonderful book, *The Three Guineas*, written in 1938, Virginia Woolf says, "As a woman I have no country. As a woman I want no country. As a woman my country is the World."

My question, after reading the narratives in this collection and thinking through my own experiences, is this: Is it easier for women to make cross-cultural transitions? Is there a global sisterhood we can draw on? Are we, as Virginia Woolf seems to imply, less tied to a country and more to people — wherever they are?

These questions are not answered easily. Generalizations are hard to make. Women usually are brought up to be caring, to cater to the social needs of the family, and to build networks around the family. The fact that they often are tied to the networks they have established might make it more difficult for them to move, unless they can take most of the network with them. But the ability they have developed for building networks, socializing, and making friends is transferable and can help them in the new culture. Women tend to bond with each other when they experience pain. Being away from home is often painful, and women may seek others in similar situations to share their sorrows.

Women seem to adapt to new cultural environments more easily than men, although, as the stories in this volume show, acculturation has its emotional costs for women. My own situation, where I have not had to give up the culture into which I was born but rather have been fortunate to "commute" between it and other cultures, has not carried such a price.

By Way of Conclusion

In her account, Alwiya Omar from Tanzania tells us how she let her children, who are now living in the United States, receive money from the tooth fairy, wear Halloween costumes, and go trick-or-treating. She does not want to deprive her children of joy and fun. She wants them to learn from the new culture they now are a part of. She goes part of the way of the old saying, "When in Rome, do as the Romans do." But she does not go all the way. She evaluates the customs, manners, and values of the new culture. Those she deems enriching for her children without threatening values of their culture of origin, she lets them freely participate in. She allows her children to help family friends decorate their Christmas tree, because, as she says, "Decorating a tree does not mean going against the Islamic tradition, even though I find it impossible to do it in my own house."

But she also tells them that Santa Claus will not come to their apartment because Christmas is part of Christianity, a religion she does not believe in. She tells her daughter, who now wears shorts, that she will not be able to do so when they get back to Zanzibar, even when the days are really hot. There are parts of her original culture she wants to adhere to and wants her children to grow up appreciating.

When my youngest son, who went to high school in the United States, visited me at Antioch College, I asked him to go for Sunday walks through the woods with me. He preferred to drive to a shopping center or to McDonald's instead, as many youngsters do in the United States, saying, "Nobody goes on Sunday walks here."

I told him, "Most Americans might not do that. But we are Norwegian." What I value most in my Norwegian heritage is the love of nature, the outdoors, hiking in the mountains, and the sight of whole families going cross-country skiing in the snow or picking mushrooms and berries in the fall.

I think this accommodating way of reacting to a new culture, letting what one finds valuable in the new culture blend with what one found valuable in the old culture, will make for smooth transitions between cultures. A person who can use this approach will feel her or his life enriched and may become truly cosmopolitan.

Unfortunately, this approach cannot always be used. If the culture one comes from is regarded as a low-status culture in the new society and one sees little likelihood of returning to the culture of origin, there will be hard pressure to give up some old values and often the native language. In such circumstances, the person in transition forever may feel culturally homeless.

132

DATE DUE